Essential Information for Every Woman & Girl
An Early Intervention and Empowerment Approach

THE DOMESTIC ABUSE PREVENTION MANUAL

Stop It Before It Starts, or From Happening Again

TANYA LANGFORD

First published by Ultimate World Publishing 2024
Copyright © 2024 Tanya Langford

ISBN

Paperback: 978-1-923123-84-7
Ebook: 978-1-923123-85-4

Tanya Langford has asserted her rights under the Copyright, Designs and Patents Act 1988 to be identified as the author of this work. The information in this book is based on the author's experiences and opinions. The publisher specifically disclaims responsibility for any adverse consequences which may result from use of the information contained herein. Permission to use information has been sought by the author. Any breaches will be rectified in further editions of the book.

All rights reserved. No part of this publication may be reproduced, stored in or introduced into a retrieval system, or transmitted in any form, or by any means (electronic, mechanical, photocopying, recording or otherwise) without the prior written permission of the author. Any person who does any unauthorised act in relation to this publication may be liable to criminal prosecution and civil claims for damages. Enquiries should be made through the publisher.

Cover design: Ultimate World Publishing
Layout and typesetting: Ultimate World Publishing
Editor: Vanessa McKay
Cover Image Copyright: Cover Artist, Robyn Udell

Ultimate World Publishing
Diamond Creek,
Victoria Australia 3089
www.writeabook.com.au

Dedication

To every woman to know your rights, and the path to be able to live as a safe and empowered woman.

Testimonials

This very important book by Tanya Langford is a major contribution to the conversation on violence against women and domestic violence in particular.

Tanya's personal story gives credibility to her work, in the world and on the page. She has lived experience of domestic violence which provides an invaluable lens with which to offer analysis, prevention and healing to others who are or have been victims of DV as well as to other educators and therapists who work in the field.

Unlike many books on this topic, Tanya's "manual" is extremely accessible and offers concrete information and skills and most importantly, a focus on prevention. In my 4 decades in this field I have rarely come across a more impactful book on DV. I would call Tanya's work both powerful and hopeful.

Anita Roberts:
Founder of Safeteen International. Canada

Domestic violence and childhood trauma often go hand in hand. The disempowered child becomes the disempowered adult and the impact is devastating. Tanya Langford has written a manual to explain all the elements of domestic violence to help any one suffering to find support. Information is power and this manual contains the information in a very factual way as well as ideas on how to move forward and how to heal the wounds.

Liz Mullinar (AM):
Founder of 'Heal For Life'. NSW. Australia

The Domestic Abuse Prevention Manual for Women and Girls is packed with so much vital information for all women and girls living with or affected by DA.

The Manual also includes so many references for help and support.

Tanya has poured her wisdom through her own journey, heart and soul into bringing this book to life so that so many women and girls can benefit, heal and break free from DA.

She is living proof that you can, and I for one am so inspired by her passion, love and courage to bring this very important topic out into the world. Thank you so much Tanya.

Catherine Wood:
Founder/Director of 'Sanctuary of Ananda', WA. Australia

'2024 Best Holistic Relationship &
Spirituality Coach Award'

This detailed and informative book is a testament to Tanya's passionate and dedicated commitment to advocating for support and empowerment of women in all walks of life who in the past or at present are victims of domestic abuse. It needs to be on everyone's book shelf.

Tanya was awarded the Zonta Club of Peel's Education Award in 2010 to help her with her university studies. She has gone from strength to strength since graduating from Edith Cowan University in 2012 as a Bachelor of Social Science.

Congratulations Tanya, you are a champion.

Nicky Hooper:
Zonta International –
Club of Peel past President. W.A. Australia

Note From The Author

The personal life experiences shared by myself and other women within this manual and expressions of innocence or guilt are our opinions and backed by actual life events. I have deliberately obscured some identifying features for both legal and moral reasons.

In telling our stories we are cognizant that we write for ourselves and our individual perspectives, and do not presume to tell the story of others, whose feelings, thoughts and memories are their own.

This book may trigger emotional reactions in some people, and specific helpline numbers are provided in the Introduction.

Contents

Dedication	iii
Testimonials	v
Note From The Author	ix
Introduction	1
My Journey To Empowerment	3
CHAPTER 1: Why Women Need This Domestic, Abuse Prevention Manual	13
CHAPTER 2: Defining The Problem of Domestic Abuse and Why It Happens	21
CHAPTER 3: How Domestic Abuse Impacts Women and Children	29
CHAPTER 4: Individual Risk Factors and The Path to Overcome	37
CHAPTER 5: Men Who Abuse Women	47
CHAPTER 6: The Path to Healing and Recovery	57
CHAPTER 7: Assertiveness Training for Safety & Early Intervention for Our Girls	69
CHAPTER 8: Living as a Safe and Empowered Woman	93
CHAPTER 9: 'Are You Ready To Date'? and 'What Does A Healthy Relationship Look Like'?	103
CHAPTER 10: Assessments and Questionnaires	111
CHAPTER 11: Resources	121
CHAPTER 12: Stories of Hope and Inspiration	127

CHAPTER 13: Gallery – Poetry, Art and Photos	143
CHAPTER 14: Afterword	165
References	167
About the Author	171
Acknowledgements	173
Speaker Bio	175

Introduction

This Manual provides an evidence-based-approach to assist women to avoid entering abusive relationships, and breaking the cycle of abuse and violence for former victims. This approach has changed my life and is what I have used to change hundreds of other women's lives. The underlying principle is:

> *'Every woman has the right to live a safe and fulfilled life with a heart full of love and have the ability to get her needs met and access to the resources and opportunities she desires, and the path to achieve personal empowerment.'*

My Journey To Empowerment

I am the oldest of six children. When I was seven years old, our family emigrated to West Australia from England (Mum, Dad and five children, one was born here a couple of years later). I learned very early on my role of taking responsibility for and looking after others, and that nothing I did was good enough to gain my mother's approval. I carried a deep sense of shame at my awareness of the problems in our parent's relationship and for the short-comings of our migrant family within the context of the small rural community we lived in. Each of these characteristics combined to create the basis of my inner self-concept, which would manifest later in life as my Inner Relationship Personality Style.

I matured early, was a successful high-achiever in school and sport, and entered my first serious relationship at 14 years of age with a 19 year old who I would remain with and get married to, until I escaped at age 21. In those seven years, I missed out on normal teen experiences because we hung out with his crowd, where I felt very insecure. In this relationship, I experienced every form of abuse and degradation, had black eyes, my front teeth smashed, and regular threats to kill me, all while maintaining an outward façade that I was okay. I was finishing high school, studying a diploma and then a professional job and part of local sporting and social groups. Looking back, I see how he had total control over me, and the total absence of avenues for me to reach out to for help. Within our wheat-belt country town culture, I knew and witnessed men abusing their partners and wives regularly and realized this was 'just how it was' and no one got involved, but inside me I knew it wasn't right and I reached a point where his treatment of me was getting worse and I knew I had to leave.

I somehow escaped in secrecy and with the assistance of the local police and my employers, I was given an immediate transfer to the city where I began my new life. I joined a professional sporting association which I dedicated myself to, which gave me a new circle of friends and I began a relationship with one of this circle. I kept the fact I was a 21 year old divorcee who had escaped domestic violence, a secret because of the stigma and shame, all which added to the shame I had already internalised as a child.

Despite some struggles with jealousy and insecurity, these couple of years were really happy for me. However, things took a turn when I discovered my then boyfriend cheating on me and leaving to be with someone else. The pain was extreme and again I was left with a feeling I was not good enough. This was the motivation for me to make the decision to go overseas, travel and have more life experiences, which I did for the next few years and thinking that within myself, I was in a good place. I was totally unaware of the unhealed trauma I had internalised from my childhood and my first abusive relationship. I had already formed an Inner Relationship Personality Style that would make it impossible for me to connect to any good, kind, decent, man and I was destined to enter my next relationship - and two more after -with men who would abuse me, manipulate me, and take advantage of that incredible characteristic I had learned in childhood, to take care of and take responsibility for others.

Over the next twenty years and the following three relationships, I re-located several times, re-married, had two children to two different fathers, which then led me to ten years in the family-court fighting two ugly custody battles and the ensuing challenges of involvement with the Child Support Agency. I regularly dealt with the police, have had to apply for Violent Restraining Orders, lived in fear, experienced stalking, harassment, and struggled on welfare. All the above has been difficult and inevitably put massive emotional strain on me and both of my children.

Over these years, there were periods when I have been single, and I have remained committed to self-improvement and trying to understand why my life was the way it was. A well-meaning friend once said to me, "it's just the bad choices you make Tanya." (why I wrote the poem *You Made Your Bed - Lie in it,* see below). I had done extensive counselling, DV programs, personal development courses, read so many books, etc., and had times where I really thought I was doing well. Despite being intelligent, fit, healthy, attractive, with a professional background, I inevitably would find myself back in another unhappy and abusive relationship and what I call The Black Hole of Hopelessness. I knew I was caught in a cycle; I knew I kept making bad choices. I kept hoping things would get better.

(I was unaware of the saying: "keep doing things the way you have been doing, and you will keep getting the same results you have been getting.").

I reached a point about 15 years ago where my real transformation commenced after I hit rock bottom and had a mini-emotional breakdown, which came after a short stint of entering another relationship and being hurt again. It hit me so hard and I think it broke into the dam of grief and pain I was holding inside. I cried most of every day and night for weeks, it was all I could do to get the kids to school, manage the few hours of dinner and showers and get them to bed (all while still dealing with harassment from the children's fathers & family court matters). During this dark period of struggle I had weekly counselling (which I cried the whole way through) and miraculously found a couple of books that were light bulb moments of self-understanding and the path I must take to change my life and break the pattern of harmful relationships. I commenced a rigorous and disciplined daily program to create emotional healing, raise my self-esteem and inner strength. I knew I had to remain relationship free and commit myself to my goals of creating a better life for myself and my kids, plus fulfill my burning desire to go to university and gain qualifications to help me use my experiences to help other women affected by abuse.

From there, I worked hard to complete the university degree I had commenced, plus bought a block of land and became an owner-builder establishing a kit-home, our forever home – no more moving!

I commenced my career path as a Family Support Officer/ Advocate assisting women and youth. I then co-founded and ran a charity organization called Safe Woman Safe Family WA for three years, and from there established my consultancy business, I Am Woman Empowerment that I now run from my home studio.

I have created three unique programs to teach women how to break the cycle of abusive relationships, plus on gaining higher self-esteem and empowerment self-defence for women and teen girl's personal safety. In addition, I enjoy facilitating regular women's retreats. In this time, I have been awarded scholarships and awards in recognition of my services to supporting women's safety and wellbeing.

Both my son and daughter are in their twenties and have moved out of our home in the past few years to live with their partners and have turned out beautiful people that I am so proud of and I share brilliant relationships with. It is the hardest burden I carry knowing of the instability, sadness and struggles they had to endure growing up. If I had not made the transformation when I did, along with creating our stable and safe home that has been their sanctuary and base these past fifteen years, I know they would carry much deeper emotional scars and things may not be going so well for them now. It is the most beautiful and special thing in the world when they say to me, "I Love you and am proud of you mum."

It is my full belief from my journey and from the many women I have assisted that until a woman has a high degree of self-love and self-value, she will continue to attract men into her life that will maintain her low levels of worth, and will experience disrespect and abuse. If a woman is carrying negative messages from her childhood, she will continue to repeat negative patterns that will bring pain and struggle. Once high self-love and value is created, the risk for abusive relationships diminishes, there is increased capacity for living a positive self-fulfilled life along with – for those who choose to seek a partner - the correlation for meeting positive, genuine, decent men, and the potential for developing safe relationships.

I began 2024 with the clear goal of creating a manual that brings together the knowledge I have gained on my journey and the tools that helped me, which are what I have incorporated into the programs I have created. I wanted to ensure more women learn how to avoid domestic abuse, as well as the much needed focus on early intervention for girls and teens.

It took me a long time, but I finally learnt to overcome those messages from my childhood and the abusive partners. I now love and value me and possess the tools to live as a safe and Empowered Woman! This is the gift that changed me and my children's lives and that I have successfully shared with hundreds of women. I know it can change your life too.

LETTER TO THE READER

Dear reader,

I would like to convey a personal **Thank-You** for purchasing this manual and I truly hope you find within information that is going to either assist you personally, as well as friends and family, and for those in the working-capacity that there will be an added depth to your understanding that will bolster how you assist women survivors of relationship abuse and how you actively contribute to sharing knowledge of gender-based abuse prevention and breaking the cycle of violence/abuse.

Creating this manual means so much to me, as it is the combination of my life journey as a survivor of childhood and multiple relationship abuse, the many aspects of my healing and self development journey, my professional path and practice experience in the last thirteen years and the hundreds of women I have either played a role in assisting their recovery from abuse or by supporting their emotional-empowerment and overall wellness. I know what I share works!

In this time, I have created and facilitated incredibly successful and unique programs for women and teen girls that have changed their lives and, in certain cases I know have saved lives. It is my hope and mission to reach as many women and girls as possible to provide the information and guidance I wish someone had given me as a young teen entering my first abusive relationship which paved the path for a large chunk of my life, and these are the same words I have been told repeatedly by other women.

The fight to end relationship abuse, domestic violence, and gender-based abuse is complex and requires many approaches. My focus is prevention for women and girls and I know that every woman who reads this manual and follows the guidelines and gets the support recommended, and commits to becoming a safe and empowered woman who loves and values herself, is a woman who will have greater protection to not enter an abusive relationship, and for previous victims, greater protection to not re-enter an abusive relationship and successfully break the cycle of violence and abuse.

The fundamental theologies I use within my programs and this manual are: ecological; attachment theory; social theory; women's rights and empowerment. I have written this manual with a feminist lens recognising the power imbalances in our societies between men and women are the basic driver of gender-based abuse and relationship abuse. However, many of the principles within can easily apply to males receiving abuse from females, also for same-sex couples, or any form of relationship abuse where a significant power and control imbalance exists, and one person in the relationship holds the power, whilst the other is forced into the submissive role.

I Welcome you on this journey- a few points I would like you to keep in mind whilst reading:

Depending on each of your lived experiences to this point, this book will have differing meaning and impacts. Please keep an open-mind, as you may be presented with certain information that creates discomfort, also there are '*biggies*', e.g.; challenges to how you currently think about yourself or others. I assure you, when this occurs, it means you are being presented with the path required to shift paradigms of thought that are keeping you stuck. It may take some time, so please sit with the discomfort and allow yourself time to process. Be gentle with yourself (it maybe you are not quite ready for certain information at this present time and that is totally okay).

For those of you who have experienced abuse this manual may trigger and bring up certain memories that are painful. Self-care is paramount, and only you carry the responsibility of ensuring you are accessing necessary professional care if that is required, and only you know what you can safely expose yourself to. Awareness is the key. (The 'Blue Knot Foundation' phone number is below and available 24/7)

To each of you, I welcome you to write this affirmation and say it repeatedly to yourself as you work through reading this manual,

"I am on the path of recovery, healing and empowerment. I am open to learning and changing. I am creating the new me who knows her rights and worthiness."

WARNING: DUTY OF CARE: If while reading this manual you realize you are currently in an abusive relationship, please contact your nearest Women's Refuge to gain advice specific to your situation, or phone your National Women's DV Helpline Australia: 1800 007 339. If you/or your children are at risk of harm, please phone the Police Aust: 131 444 or extreme immediate risk phone: 000.

For any reader who is an abuse survivor and is feeling highly triggered at any point, I recommend you phone the Blue Knot Foundation 24 Hour Helpline for Trauma Survivors: 1300 659 467. For First Nation's People you may wish to use: 13YARN: 139 276

***You Made Your Bed – Lie in it* ...**
A poem I wrote about my 'Choices'.

How often these words I have heard said, and played in my head as I lay crying on that bloodied bed. When your childhood taught you to put others first and that you have no worth, it is only natural you will end up with a man who treats you the same 'You are nothing but dirt'.

So people, please show more care when talking to women like me, because these choices link back to our 'ACES' - our families. I know this now from many years on my healing journey, I now make my choices as a woman who is FREE! *(ACES: Adverse Childhood Experiences)*

CHAPTER 1

Why Women Need This Domestic, Abuse Prevention Manual

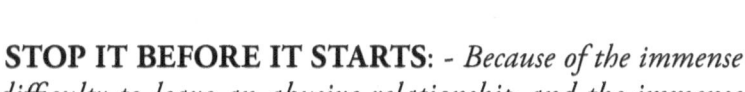

STOP IT BEFORE IT STARTS: - *Because of the immense difficulty to leave an abusive relationship and the immense heartache and suffering experienced by being in one.*

The effects of DA are felt at an individual level to women and children (and pets), but also as a broader ripple effect that impacts families, friends, services and communities, and will be explored further in Chapter 3.

I have shared with you my story in the introduction, and some testimonials from women I have worked with are shared in chapter 12, which gives you a glimpse of suffering that has been endured. Over the years, I have heard stories from hundreds of women sharing their feelings of heartbreak, betrayal, grief, shame, and the soul-crushing loss of self that is often experienced after being in an abusive relationship. For many, the pain and trauma were still so very raw and crippling, even though it had happened many years ago, for some decades ago – they still shed tears.

For each woman who is being abused, if there are children in the home, they too are being affected, whether indirectly or directly. It is now recognised that the psychological impact of a child witnessing the abuse is equal to them receiving it. Adding to this the high potential for boys to take on the abusive behaviors of their father (or other male figure) and for the girls to eventually end up in relationships with an abusive partner which is how the cycle of violence is passed on to the next generation (Routt & Anderson, 2015).

'EDUCATION IS PREVENTION AND KNOWLEDGE IS POWER'

To every woman who reads this manual and takes responsibility for what she needs to do to be safe and empowered I can vouch that you will have diminished risks of entering an abusive relationship, and that if you do, you will have a far quicker ability to recognise it and remove yourself. For any woman who has already been in an abusive relationship, the same applies. Every woman's journey to become a safe and empowered woman is different, and the time it takes will vary – for many it will be years – but the result is worth every step.

Versus

For every woman who has not read this manual and has not taken responsibility for what she needs to do to be safe and empowered, because she lacks the knowledge – her risks remain the same.

It is extremely difficult to leave an abusive relationship: it is estimated the average number of attempts to leave an abusive relationship is seven, but for some women it will be many more over years, decades, a lifetime – or for many never!

Why it is so difficult to leave an abusive relationship?

The workings of the cycle of abuse: in which the abuser shows great remorse after an abusive episode and promises he will change if the woman gives him another chance. Which creates hope that things will get better. They enter the honeymoon phase but inevitably that diminishes, and the abuse happens again.

Fear of repercussions: whether there is a high risk of physical harm, or whether there have been threats of it, for many women caught in abusive relationships, there is an extreme fear of what repercussions they will face if they attempt to leave. Post separation is identified as one period where there is the highest risk of serious harm to the woman.

Fear of how? A lack of resources, a lack of somewhere to move to: a realisation of the immense job it will be to end the relationship. The need to relocate is exacerbated if children are involved. For many, limited finances also restrict them, along with a lack of people to assist and the challenge of finding low-cost accommodation.

Feeling helpless: emotionally and mentally diminished, depression or other mental illness, physically lacking the strength.

Feeling shame: don't want people to know about the relationship problems and abuse; fear of losing friends if the truth comes out; unable to face the stigma of being labelled a failure or a single mum.

Impact on children: afraid of the negative impacts on the children of going through separation – moving house possibly and school; them having to go through the stress of shared parenting and child custody disputes and a belief that it's better for children to have both parents.

Afraid of doing property settlement: if you are married, and or have joint loans and possessions e.g.: mortgage, vehicle, business, debits, etc., the process of property settlement usually requires legal assistance and has capacity to bring heightened emotional reactions and risk of harm.

Fear of raising children as a single mother: there are genuine hardships associated with being a single mother (see Chapter 4) which are exacerbated if your partner and the father of the children has displayed abusive behavior to you, which in many cases will continue on in varied forms even after you are separated e.g. stalking or harassment and create many difficulties in co-parenting and custody issues.

Early Education as Prevention & Early Intervention for Children and Teens

Many parts of this manual needs to be taught to our children as an extreme necessity in the fight to prevent gender-based violence and domestic abuse. In chapter 7, you will see information dedicated to this purpose and be introduced to two amazing women who are mentors and inspirational friends to me who both have dedicated their lives to this mission. In the resources section I will provide you links to their websites, as well as other helpful information to help raise safe and empowered young people.

The Breaking the Cycle of Violence Evaluation Report- Evidence base to my approach.

The information presented in this manual aligns with the contents of the 10 module *Trauma Recovery and Empowerment Program* I have been delivering for the past five years. Formerly known as *The Safe Woman Safe Family 15 Week Program*. Over 100 women have been linked into this program, and about ninety have completed it.

In 2020, an evaluation was conducted in which forty-nine of the graduates participated. The findings are detailed in the report *Breaking the Cycle of Violence*, in summary:

- 100% success in remaining free from the cycle of violence or abusive relationships.
- Enhanced emotional and mental wellbeing.
- Enhanced capacity for healthy interpersonal connections.
- Enhanced feelings of empowerment and personal life satisfaction.
- Enhanced feelings of connection and reduction of feelings of isolation.

- For those with children, enhanced parenting capacity and connections.

Apart from the evidence of the evaluation report, I will share numerous testimonials from women who completed the program, as well as other women I have supported. I have stayed in contact with a great number of women I have worked with over the past thirteen years and keep track of their progress. Overwhelmingly, the positive trajectory of their lives is astounding, which also flows on to the progress of their children.

The full report can be found at www.imwomanempowerment.com/resources along with details of the program.

BREAKING THE CYCLE OF VIOLENCE

An evaluative study on the Safe Woman Safe Family W.A. 15 week Recovery and Empowerment Programs' ability to create positive and sustained changes for woman struggling to break free from the cycles, hardships and trauma, inflicted by family violence, sexual assault and other forms of gender based abuse.

Evaluation Report
December 2020

OBJECTIVES OF THIS MANUAL

- To teach life changing and lifesaving information regarding domestic abuse, which is also known as domestic violence and falls into the description of gender-based abuse, recognising the higher risks and occurrences of male to female abuse in the context of relationships (Our Watch).
- Decrease the number of women entering abusive relationships and for those women who have already been in one-or more- that they will remain safe from entering another and therefore breaking the cycle of violence.
- For women with children, this flows into enhanced parenting capacity and reduced conflict in the home or risks of exposure to abuse, whilst also reducing Intergenerational transmission of abusive or victim behaviors that occur from witnessing abuse in the family home.
- Describe the varied types of abuse, so women can recognise. Many women are confused by the terminology of domestic violence and as such do not identify themselves as being victims and do not seek help – or enter relationships without realizing abusive behaviors are already happening.
- Clarify what types of behavior are acceptable and which types are not.
- Inform about the damaging impact abusive relationships have on women and children and why it is so extremely vital to use prevention strategies and knowledge- stop it before it starts!
- Discuss the differing ways abusive men behave and categories that they fall into.
- Teach the important and life-changing skills of boundary setting; assertive communication; red flags and consent.
- Talks about harmful internal relationship personality styles to allow women the opportunity to recognise what applies to them and steps to overcome.

- Learn about minimising risk factors and where possible, take steps to change them.
- Describes the path to healing trauma; building positive self-esteem; self-worth; self-value and how to become a safe and empowered woman.
- This information should be taught to young females and males as an early intervention strategy in preventing the societal issue of gender-based abuse.

This manual will allow you to minimise and potentially avoid the chances of you entering an abusive relationship. It you find yourself in an abusive relationship, these strategies will lead to early identification and provide you with the ability to remove yourself.

CHAPTER 2

Defining The Problem of Domestic Abuse and Why It Happens

Gender-based violence is described by the World Health Organization as, "the most widespread and socially tolerated crime which violates human rights and creates a major public health problem in every country of the world." (WHO).

Terminology: within this manual I am using the term Domestic Abuse [DA] to describe every form of abuse that occurs in relationships inflicted by men to women. There are several other terms commonly used which creates confusion and sadly adds to the risks and under-reporting.

- Domestic Abuse: [DA]- every type of abuse inflicted by men to women in the context of a relationship or previous relationship.
- Domestic Violence: [DV]- as above.

- Intimate Partner Abuse/Violence: [IPA/IPV]- as above.
- Sexual Abuse/Violence: [SA/SV] - as above.
- Family And Domestic Abuse/ Violence: [FDA/FDV]-as above but including all others in the family and can present as child abuse; elder abuse; adolescent to parent abuse.
- Violence Against Women and Children: [VAWC] - as above, but in all contexts.

Definition of domestic abuse (DA): the widespread and prevalent aspect of men inflicting harmful behaviors (physical and non-physical) to women in the context of personal relationships within the domain of the home, and includes the period of separation and post separation. DA is most commonly experienced as something that escalates over time, and which creates devastating impacts at a personal and community level. Whilst there is a percentage of women who abuse men, the statistics give evidence of the gendered aspect of perpetrators and victims (AIHW, 2019A).

Gender-based abuse/violence: [GBA/GBV]: is a broader definition encapsulating all the above from the recognition we are describing abuse/violence inflicted by men to women not just in the domestic/family domain but also anywhere in the community or place of work or study etc., and from a global perspective recognising the depths of its existence in every country (Routt & Anderson, 2015).

Types of domestic abuse [DA]:

Physical violence: any act of inflicting bodily injury using any part of the body or an object: e.g. punching; head-butting; kicking; biting; pushing you into objects; choking; and more.

Physical violence to harm either property or pets: damaging motor vehicle; bashing in doors; breaking personal possessions; inflicting any form of injury to your pets; and more.

Psychological/emotional/mental abuse: verbal abuse, intense jealousy, intimidation, coercive control, constant criticism, sarcasm, threats to harm her, themselves or others, stalking and harassment in person and online. All delivered to degrade, demean, coerce, and exert fear-power and control over the victim.

Social abuse: restricting the woman from normal social activities or family connections/events as well as creating unpleasantness whenever friends or family visit, to stop them and isolating her.

Financial abuse: restricting the woman's access to funds for home and family upkeep; restricting her means of obtaining income, employment, controlling how the woman uses funds, running up debits and/or using their funds to support habits, e.g. alcohol, drugs, gambling.

Spiritual abuse: restricting the woman's activities in pursuing her religious or spiritual beliefs.

Sexual abuse: any unwanted sexual activity without the woman's consent and violating her rights; sharing of explicit sexual imagery online; sharing STDs; forcing pregnancy by irresponsible birth-control practice.

Statistics in Australia and Global (ABS, 2021-2022; Our Watch; UN Women)
[It is widely recognised that statistics relating to DA are the tip of the iceberg because of under-reporting and the real numbers are very much higher]

- Every 2 minutes in Australia, police receive a call reporting a family & domestic violence assault.
- 1 in 3 women (39%) have experienced a DA since the age of 15.
- 1 in 4 women (25%) have experienced a DA from a co-habitant partner.
- On average, one woman a week is murdered because of DA.
- In 2021/2022 - 5,606 women were hospitalised due to injuries of DA.

- 70% of women who experienced assault by a male experienced it at home.
- 1 in 2 women have experienced sexual harassment.
- Across the globe every hour, over 5 women or girls are killed by a family member.

Why does it happen?

The history of males holding power over women – patriarchy: throughout history and across cultures, males have been regarded as more powerful than women - and it is this power imbalance that is the key driver of DA and which is rooted in the structure of patriarchy. In line with this, the social structure of the family placed the man as head. Having power and control over his wife and children and entitled to expect from her: an obedient attitude of submission; to carry out domestic duties; give birth to and care for the children; to be sexually available at his request and failing to do any of these adequately, entitled him to punish her as he felt she deserved, with chastisement and beatings the commonly accepted form (Fedders, 1999).This historically has been the origin of gender roles that children are raised to conform to and in most cases, become adults carrying on these beliefs (Van Krieken et al., 2006).

Patriarchy has been entwined in our institutions, e.g., government; courts; universities; schools; religion, as well as cultural, behavioral, and attitudinal norms (Germov, 2001). Whilst many changes have occurred in the last 100 years thanks to The Feminist Movement, (e.g., women gaining the right to vote and the United Nations creating the Bills of Non Discrimination to Women and Non Violence), the fundamental masculine construct of power and control remains in our society and family homes, and is recognised as a major contributing factor to all forms of abuse inflicted by Men to Women (Van Krieken et al., 2006).

The workings of power and control: power can be identified as an individual's capacity to influence another person's attitude and behavior without fear of retaliation and is recognised as the underlying motive for abusive behaviors that men use against women. Whilst threats of, or actual acts of physical or sexual violence are visible tactics being used to exert power and control, the chart shows the varied ways an abuser can maintain fear, power, and control over a victim through experiences that are covert (Routt & Anderson, 2015).

HOW 'POWER AND CONTROL' OPERATES IN ABUSIVE RELATIONSHIPS

Threats & Coercion	Intimidation	Isolation	Controlling Finances
Creates fear of physical harm or harm to loved ones, possessions, pets or of self-harm, or of cheating on her.	Using anger & aggression to create fear & diminish her self worth & stability	Controlling what she does, who she sees, where she goes, can't access support	Stops her working, makes her ask for $, using her $, runs up debts.

Male Privilege	Emotional Abuse	Using their Children	Minimize & Justify
Treats her like servant, 'King of Castle', makes all decisions, forces her to have sex when it suits him.	Name calling, put downs, humiliation, makes fun of her, blames her for every thing that goes wrong, her feelings are ignored	Turning them against her, harming them to hurt her, using visitation to harass her, allowing them to be rude to her & misbehave	No responsibility for anything they do wrong.

Confusion regarding the definitions of DA-DV-IPV-FV

The widely used definition of domestic violence (DV) has created vast confusion over the years, with many women not seeking help and not accessing support because of their belief they are not being physically hurt so it does not fit in the category of DV, and for men – they also may not realize the behaviors they are inflicting on their partners is classified as abuse and actually breaking the law.

Confusion in attitudes regarding what constitutes abuse and victim-blaming.

The 2021 National Community Attitudes Survey Report (NCAS) proves major problems in Australia with across the board misunderstandings shown by men, women and young people regarding what behaviors constituted abuse and which did not; e.g. 54% saying DA is a normal stress reaction; 40% saying men and women equally perpetrate; 34% mistrust women's allegations, and most of those interviewed did not believe violence against women was a problem in their community (NCAS).

Tied into the rigid historical constructs of patriarchy and gender roles lies attitudes regarding how a good woman, lady, wife, partner should behave and certain forms of her behavior or not performing her duties could give her Husband/Partner grounds to use forceful physical harm to her. This is called victim blaming. In certain sub-groups, communities, cultures – the male will be applauded for demonstrating his masculine power and control.

This confusion is also reflected by our young people. Research undertaken in schools and universities confirms both males and females are grossly unaware of what behaviors are classified as abuse that are punishable by the police and the courts, e.g. normalization of violence and making excuses for abuse – such as 'being drunk' or 'being provoked'.

> In the Keeping Us Safe **Program,** I ran in 2021 at a local High School for approximately 1,000 Girls from Year 7 to Year 11 this confusion was highly reflected in the data we collected.

Indigenous Australians and other cultures living in Australia have grown with a differing view regarding a man's rights to treat his partner/wife in a certain way, and these may not be in line with the legal definitions and rulings that will be enforced by the police and the courts.

Intergenerational transmission of abusive and violent behavior to women:

Children raised in homes where they are regularly exposed to DA between their parents/carers are highly likely to develop a normalisation of male to female abusive interactions. This is how the cycle of violence carries from one generation to the next, and another depiction of the strong transmission of traditional gender roles, e.g., the male holds power over the female. The result is highly predictive that these boys will use abusive behaviors in their future relationships, and that the female has the probability of entering a relationship with an abusive partner (this is compounded if a girl also has experienced abuse in childhood) (Routt & Anderson, 2015).

Other social influences:

There are many aspects present in our society that perpetuate the traditional belief system of males being powerful and having control over females who are viewed and treated as inferior and who should behave as submissive and perform their duties obediently; in addition – that demean and disrespect women by sexual objectification aimed for men's gratification:

(Example presented in the Youtube clip: 'Be a Lady They Said' by Cynthia Nixon)
YouTube.

In addition:
- **Fashion Industry** – sets standards of how women should look and dress to be sexy.
- **Music Industry** – certain genres have highly sexually explicit and violent lyrics and videos, that are promoting men's sexual objectification of women, as well as female artists who use their sexuality to promote their popularity.
- **Pornography** – the over-riding depiction enforces male domination of women, and there has been an escalation in recent years showing violent sexual behaviors to women. Recognising also that in recent years, the online accessibility creates a high influence on young people's concepts of male and female treatment to each other.
- **Gaming** – increased presence of males dominating women sexually and also how the creators ensure sexualized appearance of women.
- **Social Norms** – the stereotypical male wolf-whistle from any group of men if an attractive woman (or girl) walks by.
- **Violent Media** – exposure to media has long been recognised as a direct link to heightened aggression (Huesmann, 2010).

Prevention education to minimise the risk of experiencing DA aims to ensure a clear understanding of the varied types of abuse and exactly what forms of behavior constitute an action that is defined as punishable within our legal system. This will assist you in protecting your rights and keeping you safe.

CHAPTER 3

How Domestic Abuse Impacts Women and Children

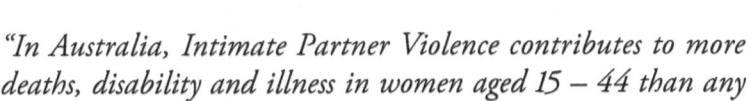

"In Australia, Intimate Partner Violence contributes to more deaths, disability and illness in women aged 15 – 44 than any other preventable risk factor." (Our Watch, 2023).

"Women post-separation where domestic abuse has existed have "… a violent crime victimization rate that is higher than that of any other." (Van Krieken et al., 2006).

Domestic Abuse [DA] is a serious and widespread social problem with devastating physical, psychological, and economic consequences for victims. While men are more likely to experience violence from strangers and in a public place; women are most likely to know the perpetrator (often their current or a previous partner) and the violence usually takes place in their home (AIHW), 2019a).

Impacts of domestic abuse on women: for those of us working in assisting women who have been impacted by family and domestic abuse —past or current - observe their ongoing hardship and struggles. Whether physical or other abuse has been experienced, these women are living with trauma and suffering which predisposes them to further issues such as: mental illnesses; substance abuse; financial hardship; parenting difficulties; poor family management; unstable living situations & often homelessness (Moore). There is significant research that shows a bi-directional causal relationship between exposure to FDA and persistent mental health challenges (Trevillion et al.) Many are dealing with multiple agencies, i.e., family court; child custody & parenting disputes; Child Support Agency; Centrelink; Department of Child Protection Services and more.

Often, these women live with ongoing threats from former partners, and many are forced to regularly engage with police and district courts, where VROs (Violence Restraining Orders) are necessary to try to keep them safe. For these women and their children, there is a constant state of high vigilance & constant fear. The combination of unresolved trauma and the complexities of managing their own lives as well as their children's lives, mixed with constant feelings of unworthiness, places many women at high risk to themselves and others with poor hopes for improved futures.

Abuse related trauma: neuroscience confirms that the trauma created by DA (heightened if the woman also had child abuse trauma) affects a person's brain function and can have long lasting impacts, on a person's emotional & behavioral patterns; creating dysfunction in their lives and relationships. If left unprocessed and unhealed, this trauma will continue to wreak havoc on relationships with children, friends, family & current or future partners. Healing from trauma differs for every individual and can take many years and a wide range of treatments and will be discussed more in Chapter 6.

Impacts of domestic abuse on children: there are a wide range of impacts on children being raised in homes where DA is occurring, which vary according to the age of the children and the types of abuse (Routt & Anderson, 2015):

Physical harm: there is a correlation between abuse of the mother and the children. Many times where physical abuse is being inflicted on the mother, young children in proximity also receive harm. Older children can be harmed for getting involved in any conflict that is occurring.

Emotional impacts and behaviors: exposure to DA affects the developing brain and this maladaptation can leave a lasting detrimental impact on the children of DA survivors, whether they witnessed the violence firsthand (Callaghan, Alexander, Sixsmith & Fellin, 2018). Examples of the impacts: highly emotionally reactive extreme behaviors in the home and at childcare settings/schools; learning and development milestones not being reached; inability to concentrate in classroom; separation anxiety; bed-wetting; nightmares; at-risk behaviors; self-harming; alcohol and drug use; juvenile criminal activity and more.

Intergenerational transmission of abuse: children who observe abuse between their parents have a high probability of repeating these behaviors when they are older and enter relationships, this can present as boys displaying controlling and aggressive behaviors whilst girls displaying submissive and victim patterns of relating (Howard & Abbott, 2013).

Adolescent violence in the home (AVITH): is an aspect of intergenerational transmission where the adolescent displays abusive/violent behaviors to the parent whom they have witnessed being the victim (in most cases the mother), often using the same physical violence and verbal degradation as they witnessed. This problem manifests further when parents separate, and statistics show single mothers as being the highest number receiving abuse. The feelings of pain, shame, guilt, hopelessness are intense, and every day is a struggle- with many of these women developing depression and other mental health issues. Whilst any gender or age can be the perpetrator, the oldest boy of the family represents the highest risk, which can tie into his belief, "he is now the Man of the family," (Anderson & Routt, 2015).

In Australia, 1 out of every 8 police calls for family violence involve a young person as the perpetrator (VRCFV).

> I have extensive experience in the area of AVITH, having run the Step Up intervention program (Routt & Anderson, 2015) and conducted my own research, plus partnered in a national project. The extent of the seriousness of this risk and the lack of adequate assistance is a major concern. The link will be in the resources section.

Homelessness: youth make up 21% of Australia's homeless number and it is recognised many of these are the outcome of unstable/broken families where they witnessed/experienced F&DV, or from situations of single mothers re-partnering particularly in blended families, or when mother has a new baby with the new partner and the young person is either not being treated well or does not feel they belong (AIHW, 2021).

When relationships breakdown and the impacts of leaving:

There are always heightened emotions and stress when dealing with the many aspects of leaving an abusive relationship – reorganising lives, living situations and potential legalities which apply to both parties. In addition, where children are involved, it can cause them to be distressed, unsettled and confused. This is a period known to present escalated risks for safety for women and children.

If children are from the relationship, the major tasks and agency involvement are:

- Separation and divorce, property settlement - lawyers.
- Child custody matters / possible involvement of family court (which involves the Anglicare Family Relationship Centre,

initially), Child Support Agency, Centrelink, and in all cases possible involvement of police and the courts for violence restraining orders, plus relevant health and mental health services.
- Possibly relocate, and move children to a new school.

If no children from the relationship, the major tasks and agency involvement are:

- Separation, divorce, property settlement – lawyers.
- Police and the courts for violence restraining orders, plus relevant health and mental health services.
- Possibly relocation.

Escalated risk of harm: the post separation period presents 70% of reported injuries, and for many women this period can run into years in which they deal with harassment, stalking and threats to destabilise attempts to move forward in life. Women post-separation where DA has existed, become part of a population group which has "… a violent crime victimization rate that is higher than that of any other," (Van Krieken et al., 2006).

The extreme level of this risk is sadly demonstrated where the women and in some cases the children, have been murdered shortly following the separation, as the "likelihood of being killed increases by more than 30 fold," (Levesque, 2001). Data collected between 2010 and 2018 confirmed 311 women had lost their lives because of intimate partner homicide, and the majority occurred after the relationship had ended (ANROWS, 2019).

Impact on children: the fall-out of all that is occurring during and following the period of separation has a significant effect on the physical and emotional wellbeing of the children. Anglicare Family & Relationship Centres are the front-line organisation in Western Australia for mums and dads to gain assistance in creating parenting plans and dispute-resolution to work through disagreements regarding the arrangements of shared-parenting. In addition, they are the required first step before being able to lodge applications with the Family Court of WA. Anglicare has done substantial research over the years, and confirmed that children can adjust well where both parents show respect and amicably work to create the new living arrangements and wellbeing of the children (Anglicare, WA). However, the reality for a woman who has escaped an abusive relationship is that she will experience extreme stress and harassment whilst trying to sort through child-custody matters and so will the children, and this can continue for many years.

Single Mothers and financial hardship: single mothers are recognised as one of the most disadvantaged groups in Australia, and this is compounded for mothers in minority groups, e.g. Disability; CALD; Indigenous; GLBTQ (Van Krieken et al., 2006). Child poverty in single parent families sits at 20 – 25% and this impacts directly onto the children in a multitude of ways. By taking into consideration the range of stressors at play for a woman with children escaping an abusive relationship, without a good network of support there is heightened risks that reduce her capacity to provide a safe and supportive environment for the children, which is a predictor for numerous negative outcomes in children's development and loss of opportunities (Moore, 2008).

Whilst there are exceptions of single mothers with great support and resources behind them the vast majority face hardship. Depending on the woman's earning capacity plus the age and the specific needs of the children, along with child-care requirements and costs, it is a struggle for many single mothers to find well-paying employment whilst providing optimum care to children. Many single mothers are forced to rely on welfare (Single Parent Pension) which is minimal. Depending on the father's employment (or lack of), what is received through child support payments can assist and make a big difference to living situations for single mothers and the children. However, if the father is unemployed (and/or doing cash jobs) the monthly base-rate will be paid, which is currently $9.98 a week or $519.00 a year (Services Australia webpage) this provides very little change to their struggle.

> In my personal experience, both fathers avoided and hated paying Child Support and used varied ways of hiding their true income. They seemed to resent whatever amounts they had to pay and it created great animosity which would be vented at me and often onto the children at visitation time. Many women I have worked with share a similar experience.

Homelessness: Leaving DA is the leading cause of homelessness for women and children in Australia. In 2021 – 2022, 72,900 women sought help from specialist homelessness services (AIHW, 2022). A lack of affordable rental accommodation and insufficient emergency housing, e.g.: hostels, has resulted in a greater number of mothers and their children either staying in abusive relationships, or sleeping in their cars or tents with bleak future prospects.

Long term implications: in Australia over the past decade, there has been a 6.6% rise in homeless figures of women in the 55+ years old age bracket, and this is now recognised as the fastest growing cohort (Human Rights website). Many are sleeping in cars, couch-surfing and accessing emergency services to meet basic needs. I personally know a number of former clients in this situation.

If we look at the factors behind this dismal situation in many cases this is the long-term impact of DA and relationship breakdown, separation and divorce; particularly for women who were raising children and struggling on welfare with little financial assistance from the father. As the children get older and leave school, many still rely on their mother to give them accommodation (whether they have work, potentially on welfare also). When the time arises where it is just the woman entering older years, relying on welfare or the aged pension- no savings or superannuation, her budget very often cannot manage and there is not enough low-cost rental accommodation available.

Re-partnering after leaving an abusive relationship:

A woman with or without children who has left an abusive relationship has a much higher risk of re-entering another abusive relationship than a woman who has not experienced abuse (Zohra, Jackeb, 2018). In addition, if she has children there exists a higher risk they will experience abuse from her new partner. (This risk exists also for the children if their father has re-partnered when they have visitation at his home).

Children at-risk entering foster care:

All the above factors exert extreme pressures and unfortunately diminish parenting capacity, which then creates a vast range of risks for the safety and well-being of the children. At present in Australia approximately 46,000 children have been removed by the Department of Communities and placed in foster care (AIHW, 2021).

CHAPTER 4

Individual Risk Factors and The Path to Overcome

This chapter holds such importance to achieving this manual's goal of educating women as a **tool** for the prevention of entering into or enduring abusive relationships. It is my hope you will gain insights and knowledge that you can use as the basis for your path ahead. May I suggest this is a good time to do the following self-assessments in Chapter 10 to assist you in recognising which risk factors and personality characteristics are relevant to you as you read through, and also having a note-pad to make a list of what you recognise, as this will be important for your future path of **recovery, healing and personal development.**

(Please go to Chapter 10 and complete the: (1) *ACES Questionnaire*; (2) Emotional Abuse; (3 a & b) *My Self Esteem Rating and Varied Influences*)

1) Childhood adversity: our childhoods and how we were cared for hold deep significance to understanding ourselves and the type of relationships we are highly likely to find ourselves in. Until we recognise the patterns of how we function and take the required steps to modify what is unhealthy – we will continue to be at risk of attracting into our lives men with particular sets of characteristics that will manifest themselves as harmful abuse.

The ACE results: [*Adverse Childhood Experiences*] once you have completed this questionnaire, please go through the results and tie in with your knowledge or memory. Did your childhood contain any of the following: dysfunction; abuse (any of the types); abandonment; neglect; harsh treatment; lack of nurturing; parental issues, (conflict, violence, addictions, mental health, other serious debilitating health issues); was it necessary for you to take on excessive responsibility (house-duties, caring for siblings, caring for parent), and attachment styles of either – avoidant, ambivalent or disorganised (see below).

If you recognise even just one of these factors, or a combination, it is highly probable this will have impacted on your early years emotional development and affected the hard-wiring of your brain where the earliest foundation of self-perception is formed. This begins when you are a baby and continues in early infancy, and this early inner self belief is of immense significance throughout your whole life, and particularly relevant to our 'Inner Relationship Personality Style'(IRPS) and the type of relationships you will find yourself in.

Attachment theory: the findings of Thomas Bowlby refers to the care you received, and the relationship you had with your mother (or other main care-giver) in the first 2 -3 years of life, as the 'Attachment Style' which becomes internalised and creates your inner self beliefs. As you will see in the table below, this gives reliable predictions of future personality characteristics; vulnerabilities; life outcomes and the type of relationships you will find yourself in (Berk, 2000).

Implications of Attachment Theory

Attachment-Style	Inner Self-Belief	Personality Characteristics	Types of Relationships
SECURE Warm, comforting, Responsive	**I'M OK & YOU'RE OK**	Healthy and balanced Self Esteem;; Positive outlook; well adjusted; Reliable; Trusting	Seeks a healthy and balanced Partner, lots of good friends
INSECURE/avoidant Resent, neglect, Limited nurturing	**I'M OK & YOU'RE NOT OK**	High anxiety; defensive; exiled; Don't need anyone; self-harm; Self soothe with alcohol/drugs	Narcissistic likelihood; Bully; Blaming; Struggle to make friends
INSECURE/anxious Unstable, chaotic Inconsistent care	**I'M NOT OK & YOU'RE OK**	Low confidence; sensitive; Hypervigilant; anxious; depressed; Victim; fear abandonment	Likely to be bullied; Codependent: high chance of being abused.
DISORIENTED / DISORGANIZED Severe abuse, Neglect & Trauma	**I'M NOT OK & YOU'RE NOT OK**	Unworthy; insecure; inner anger; Low trust; defensive; insecure; Addictions; likely end up in prison or engaged in criminal activity	Don't fit in well, will find others similar as friends & abusive relationships; children will be same

Our inner self-beliefs represent what we internally have decided is our worthiness rating – this feeds into our self-esteem rating and is the blueprint that will last our whole life (unless we take action to change it), and can hold a combination of negative aspects, e.g.: core hurts (unseen, unheard, unlovable, unimportant); shame; guilt; inferiority; worthless; self loathing; hatred. These aspects become part of us and some may be externally evident such as shyness and insecurity. Whilst others we can hide away inside and cover up with our survival-strategies, e.g.: over achiever; class clown; super kind & sweet. However, they can surface at other times such as if we are highly stressed, and are intricately woven into our Inner Relationship Personality Style (IRPS) without us even realising, and preventing us from forming happy and safe relationships, whilst raising our likelihood of abusive relationships.

2) Unhealthy inner relationship personality styles that put women at RISK:

CO-DEPENDENCY: (also known as *Women Who Love Too Much*) Women who attract men that have issues/problems (e.g., addictions, debt, struggling in life) so they can pour all their love and attention into helping them. The pay-off to the woman is feeling needed. Usually these women have hurtful childhoods where their own needs were not met and they have a lot of inner healing required – however it is too scary to look within, so they prefer to invest their efforts into their partner. In her book *Women Who Love Too Much* Robyn Norwood describes this as an addiction that affects thousands of women around the world, and that until a woman does serious personal work in recovery it will be impossible for her to break the cycle of choosing men who will harm her(Norwood, 2008).

RESCUERS, HELPERS and GIVERS:,: (similar to above) – these women's homes are filled with rescue animals, rescue kids from other families, they are often stalwarts as volunteers helping at varied charities, and similarly they attract partners who have lots of problems – who are not reliable and stable and present risks to the woman and her children.

INNER UNWORTHINESS, GUILT and SHAME: this can present in women who are struggling in life, and also in women who appear externally to have it all together with great jobs, homes, etc. These women will not be able to relate with a good, safe and trustworthy man, but will find themselves with men who do not treat them well and this reinforces that inner belief system.

MOTHER-WOUND: women whose mothers were unloving and cruel, carry deep core-wounds and generally find it very difficult to develop a healthy relationship with a decent man. Their deep inner pain along with the many feelings of unworthiness, will make it difficult to connect and trust. There is high potential to end up in relationships without a solid foundation and with men with their own issues. Impatient & uncompassionate partners are quick to anger if their needs are not being met, which creates potential for a woman to be harmed even further. There is high chance that her mother also had this wound, and that if she has a daughter, it will inevitably be repeated and passed on.

INSECURE and CLINGY: women whose childhoods were unstable and where they learnt that they could never rely on anything are likely to have inner personality characteristics of insecurity, high anxiety, constant need for validation and low self-worth. They have a high likelihood of being bullied at school and potential for ending up with a controlling and abusive partner. Because of the other characteristic of severe fear of abandonment, these women will find it very difficult to leave an abusive relationship.

INSECURE PROTAGONIST: similar to the above, with the development of a strategy for attention - even if it is harmful attention. These women seek opportunities to instigate arguments or create jealousy in their partner to provoke their anger and create explosions of intense emotions and potential violence to either the woman or to a third party. This woman knows how the cycle of violence works and uses it for the payoff of the honeymoon period of receiving apologies and gifts. This is where she also gets her validation of feeling loved and needed.

CONSTANT NEED FOR EXCITEMENT and DRAMA: if a woman has grown up with a difficult, abusive, chaotic childhood, this is what feels familiar to her so it almost impossible for her to enter a relationship with a man who presents as quiet, nice and stable (Norwood). This woman will seek out the bad boy image with associated risks, and the inevitable harm that she knows will come, because it is what she feels is normal and where she satisfies her need for chaos.

PASSIVE AGGRESSIVE and USE OF SILENT TREATMENT: many women who have grown up with abuse and chaotic homes witnessing a lot of conflict have extreme difficulty communicating their feelings, particularly their angry feelings. It is common to use submissive behaviors with underlying simmering rage. They have a high potential to end up with an abusive partner and during conflict they emotionally shutdown and want to isolate and will avoid any communication for extended periods. These characteristics are all signs of deep childhood trauma and possibly how they survived as children. However, these are not aligned with how individuals in healthy relationships communicate and handle disputes. In unsafe relationships these have the potential of further angering and creating greater risk for harm.

LOW SELF ESTEEM: (refer to the results of your self-assessment (3a)). If you recognise you have low self-esteem, it is highly likely you also have difficulty setting boundaries and this combination creates a major risk factor.

Other characteristics that present a risk factor: there is a vast range of emotional and behavioral characteristics that can be present in a woman's inner relationship personality style that create risk and are areas that require assistance and support to overcome: highly sensitive and reactive; timid; unable to speak true feelings; self-sacrificing; difficulty saying no; intimacy issues; promiscuity issues, etc.

If you recognise and identify with any of the above characteristics this holds significance to:

a) Types of relationships you attract.
b) How you function in those relationships.
c) Your feelings and wellbeing.
d) Your safety.

3) Your knowledge of domestic abuse: your understanding of what is and is not is a protective factor or a RISK! You cannot practice personal safety and set healthy boundaries if you are unable to assess when you are being abused. Your understanding of normal is impacted by your childhood family and other settings such as school etc. and what you have been exposed to in your community. Lack of this knowledge and failure to recognise red flags is a serious risk factor.

4) Risks to indigenous women: indigenous women experience DA at much higher rates and their risk of hospitalization is 15 X Higher (AIHW, 2019). It is recognised that different cultural attitudes exist which create difficulties in providing prevention, support and assistance. Risks are known to be even higher in remote communities.

5) Risks to CALD, refugees and migrant women: higher risks exist for these women and the presence of differing cultural attitudes to rights is an obstacle, as well as lacks of support and for some, inability to speak English compounds vulnerability and isolation. Another commonly seen risk factor for Women who have obtained entry to Australia through a marital visa arrangement, is that she may be experiencing all forms of abuse but avoids seeking medical or legal assistance due to him using threats regarding residency, e.g. cancellation of visa or deportation. In cases where women access emergency accommodation in a refuge, due to their ineligibility for welfare financial assistance they often face no path forward apart from returning to the abuser (Vaughn, 2018).

6) Risks to women with disabilities: 15.9% of women with a disability or long term health condition reported abuse in the last twelve months, compared to 4.3% for women without (ABS, 2021-2022). Depending on a woman's type of disability and care requirements, varying levels of DA risk exist. In situations where a woman's husband/partner is the main carer – and is using abusive treatment to her, she is highly vulnerable and depending on what other services she is linked with there may be limited avenues to reach out for help and limited alternative options.

7) Risks to transgender and gender diverse: higher rates of abuse exist (Hill, 2020). Regardless of gender, in any relationship between two people if a power imbalance exists there is potential for all the different types of abuse to occur.

8) Risks to women with addictions to alcohol and/or drugs: whether in a relationship or looking to enter one, any woman who has an addiction to alcohol and/or drugs puts herself at risk of abusive treatment, particularly when under the influence and her functioning is impaired. These risks are heightened if her partner also has an addiction, particularly any situations of conflict where escalated emotional reactions occur and lack of capacity to self-control (Routt & Anderson, 2015).

9) Risks to women who have already been in an abusive relationship: it is recognised that any woman who has already been in an abusive relationship, has a highly escalated rate of entering another (Zohre et al., 2018), and this risk is further compounded if she also experienced child-hood abuse. If this woman has children, she is known to be in the cohort of highest risks for victimisation (Van Krieken et al., 2006).

10) Risks to women who are experiencing financial hardship: there are multiple intersecting disadvantages and **risks** for a woman living with financial hardship, which are compounded if she is a single mother, all which create high risk for entering an abusive relationship (Van Krieken et al., 2006)

Reflecting on Your Results

How many of these risk factors apply to you? May this manual be the guide for you to learn how to overcome and minimise risks, modify harmful inner relationship personality style qualities, access the path to healing trauma if required; raise knowledge and create individual path to becoming a safe and empowered woman.

> **HOW TO OVERCOME AND MINIMISE RISK FACTORS**
>
> - Recognise the trauma you are carrying from adversity in your childhood and/or other abusive relationships – seek the path of healing and recovery as will be described in this manual.
> - Recognise if your childhood damaged your inner self-perception and you have developed unhealthy inner relationship personality style characteristics – seek the path to help you change.
> - Commit to your personal development and building your levels of self worth and self esteem with the goal of becoming a safe and empowered woman.
> - Inform yourself with all the forms of DA, know red flags; types of abusers and their tactics.
> - Learn how to set effective boundaries using assertive language.
> - Know your rights as a woman and be prepared to create standards of respect in your life.
> - Set the bench-mark of what you will and will not have in your life.
> - Know what a healthy relationship is and commit to never settling for anything less. Learn to practice extreme caution if commencing dating and take time to do necessary 'checks' and remember your standards.

- Know that you cannot change a person, but you can create change in you.
- Be aware that sometimes we have to make big choices and take radical steps to remove negative and toxic people from our lives for us to move forward in creating a better future for ourselves and our children.
- Be aware that when you are making these changes in your life, some people will object because they benefit from you not advancing your empowerment.

"I am not what happened to me, I am what I choose to become."
(Carl Gustav Jung)

CHAPTER 5

Men Who Abuse Women

In this Chapter we are looking at the varying categories of abusive men. In each of these categories you will find men with particular Inner Relationship Personality Styles (IRPS) that predispose them to seek out certain types of IRPS Women that will enable them to operate to their optimum level of satisfaction and get their needs met, with detriment to the woman and highly unlikely to provide her a healthy relationship. We will then learn about red flags which are an essential safety tool, as well as understanding **'the cycle of violence and abuse'** and how abusive men continue their patterns of harmful behavior to women, as well as some of the commonalities shared between them.

Influential factors: just as there are (IRPS) and category types we recognise when working with women who have been through abusive relationships, that have capacity to heighten their risk of being abused as described in Chapter 4, the same applies when examining men who abuse women. The same recognition of how aspects of childhood impact early personality development and sense of self applies to men and how their IRPS will operate.

When a male infant-child-adolescent's life has been impacted by abuse and all those harmful aspects listed in Chapter 3 – he too will experience maladaptation in his brain development from trauma, which if untreated and unhealed, will create negative influence to his life and every relationship. In addition, referring to the attachment theory table in chapter 4, the lack of loving and consistent care in the first two years of life will create a significant impact on his future capacity to form meaningful relationships and the characteristics in his IRPS.

When considering the development of self in boys, a range of other influences are at play e.g.: if he had a father/significant other male who treated him harshly from the belief, "boys have got to be toughened up" (likely how he was raised); other toxic-masculinity messages such as "boys don't cry", "don't be a sissy", and gendered messages of masculine power that underpins an attitude that sees females as inferior. This will also be influenced by his own mother and the direct gender-based messaging she provided, as well as how he saw her treated by his father or other men (Biddulph, 1997).

If a boy grows up in a household where he witnesses his mother being abused and disrespected, this will be a dominant contributing factor to how he will treat females in his relationships. For many boys, this effect presents early as AVITH (Adolescent Violence in the Home) where abusive behavior is directed at the mother (Routt & Anderson, 2015). Without early intervention, the realization that abuse gives power and control will become an internalised strategy that is highly likely to be woven into his (IRPS) that has the potential to be hidden initially only to emerge once a relationship is established.

Other influences on how a boy grows to become a man who uses abusive behavior in his relationships with women can be determined with the ecological theory, e.g., family structure; living conditions; socio-economic situation; neighborhood; culture; religion; laws;

government ideologies and more (Garbarino, 1985) – all which link back into the influences of patriarchy as discussed in Chapter 2.

Categories of men who abuse women:

In view of what has been discussed, here is a listing of categories that are recognised as having great potential to inflict harm and abuse on women. In each of these categories, every aspect of domestic abuse can present, and the categories can often overlap, e.g., addicted and violent.

The emotional predator: (Narcissistic Traits) – Has a sixth sense of how women operate and will play to your wounds and vulnerabilities, e.g., been dumped, previous abuse, lonely, insecure. They are chameleons and can be whatever you need them to be. They will pick up hints of your interests and conform their lives to appear in tune. Once they feel they have you hooked their real fun begins. These men gain pleasure from mind games and inflicting mental-suffering. They have no empathy and enjoy domination.

The covert narcissist: portray themselves as gentle-souls, may be wounded and vulnerable, and dedicated to the path of enlightenment – they will reel you in by appealing to your sense of empathy. They are a wolf in lamb's clothes as once they have your trust the mind games begin. They delight in your confusion as they twist your feelings or concern back on you, depicting you as unbalanced. They feel entitled to dominate you and have no regard for your pain.

The addicted: (attracts a co-dependent woman who loves too much)- in many situations a woman can commence dating a man with an addiction that he keeps a secret, or she may think she is with a fun-loving party guy and have great attraction to him. His addiction could be: drugs, alcohol, pornography, gambling, sex and many more. This type of man has a sixth sense for women who are co-dependent, just as she has for men with problems. Because she falls into love and the relationship so fast, and immediately begins her compulsive care-giving with the belief she can fix him, he can continue his addiction (and whatever negative and abusive behaviors co-exist) because she will be so invested in him and keeping the relationship going, even when she knows the truth – her addiction is the relationship.

The violent 'Jekyll & Hyde': can initially present as very charismatic and charming, giving you lots of attention and treats. They are luring you into their web. Once you are there, the real Mr Hyde creeps out with explosions of anger. They will confront you with their rage to terrify you and exert their power and control, e.g.: jealousy and accusations, blaming, shaming, ridiculing, verbal and physical abuse with manipulations to stop you telling anyone or getting help. They know how to play the cycle of violence to win you back with promises.

The permanent clinger: (Attracts a Co-dependent Woman Who Loves Too Much) is a needy and victim-based man. He will give a woman a lot of attention with the expectation he will get all of his needs met. They are jealous of other people in your life and turn the tables to ask you to give up your life and make them your focus. They convince you they have been wounded and you can heal them with your love. They may use threats of self-harm or eternal wounding to keep you trapped in the relationship using your compassion to stop you leaving.

The hidden secrets/con man: men who have undisclosed secrets e.g.: affairs, same-sex partners, children, addictions, debts, criminal histories, and other things they purposefully hide from you. They are skilled liars with the ability to twist anything you query to make you look like you are jealous and insecure. They will worm their way into your life and your heart and gain your trust, which in some situations also poses risks to your financial security and your credibility or reputation.

The mentally ill: he may look good on the outside, but after a while of dating serious issues emerge. Depending on the diagnosis and what treatments he is supposed to be accessing, escalated behaviors and risk can present if he stops taking his medications or accessing the professional prescribed treatment. Some can be manipulative using emotional blackmail to stop you from leaving them. They may threaten to take their lives or do extreme harm.

The emotionally unavailable: these are men who are married, separated, dating or may have an ex they still have an occasional connection with – who lure you in with love bombing and declarations of how wonderful you are, however the twist is that they have something stopping them from fully committing to you. They may also be men very preoccupied with work, study, sport or hobbies that take first place with the expectation you will be there when they want you.

The man seeking parenting and shelter: (Single Mums are the Jackpot!) – he may be very appealing and have wonderful, seductive power aimed at getting into your home and your bed! Once there he will play on your kindness and pity, because he is going through a rough patch needs somewhere to stay just for a few days, which can easily stretch out. He will use every bit of assistance and mothering you can give him. These men usually have a track record of inability to hold down jobs, accommodation or any form of stability and may also have a range of other issues, e.g., debts, addictions, criminal activities, criminal histories and in addition, the risks of harm that can present when you seriously want them to leave.

THE SEXUAL PREDATOR (TYPE A) and (TYPE B):

Type A - the player: he will charm you, love-bomb and shower you with affection and adoration. The truth is, he really has no intention of forming a relationship – his only goal is to have sex with you and he will work so very hard at breaking down any resistance or hesitancy you show. Once he has claimed his prize he may tag you along for a period, during which it is likely he is seeing other women as well. As soon as he is bored he will discard you and move on for his next prey. He is a compulsive liar with zero empathy for any emotional pain you go through when he disappears.

Type B - the pervert: he targets single mums with daughters (ages according to his taste, which may also target boys). He will charm you and use every tactic to gain your affection and trust, as Goal #1 is for you to invite him into your home-life and introduce him to your children. Goal #2 is to nestle into your home life, have sleepovers and build on his relationship with your children. He will present as a family loving and kid friendly fun guy who makes your life easier and helps around the home to take the load off you. Goal #3 is to spend time alone with your child/children. His intent is PURE EVIL and will bring pain and destruction to you and your children.

Red flags:

Warning Signs are an important early intervention, safety and abuse prevention tool that all women need to know about, because they can save you from remaining connected to a man who poses great risk to you, which will worsen the longer you stay in contact. It is important for you to also give thought to which red flags are deal breakers, e.g., no warning – no discussion – just clear communication you wish no further contact. This also requires ensuring you return any property of his you may be in possession of; deleting all social media connections; blocking his phone number; taking every step possible for your personal safety and to not hesitate in seeking assistance from the police if this person continues to pursue you.

- Using aggression or verbal abuse is an urgent red flag of danger.
- Jealously/possessiveness: of your time spent with others, particularly 'males'.
- Speaks disgustingly about his 'ex': this is an early indicator of his character.
- Love bombing: coming on too fast with excessive texting, phone calls, gifts.
- Disrespects your opinions: makes fun of things you say, or interrupts.
- Derogatory language: to you at home in private; whether against your family or work colleagues; speaking or acting disrespectfully to you in public; towards a person serving you in a coffee shop or other venue; describing persons of other race-culture-ability.

- Inappropriate affection to other women: or disrespectful sexually suggestive language.
- Isolating tactics: trying to prevent you having contact with others, e.g.: socially / family / other.
- Poor emotional regulation/anger control: displaying anger when under pressure or is annoyed. Highly reactive to any form of criticism.
- Alcohol abuse and related drunken behavior: early detection of an excessive alcohol dependency spells trouble, in addition, unruly and inappropriate behavior when drunk.
- Drug use: early detection of illegal drug use.
- Trying to control how you look and dress: making negative comments about what you are wearing, or trying to get you to look a certain way, eg: "more sexy". This extends to every aspect of your appearance e.g., hair and makeup.
- Monitoring you (a form of 'Stalking'): whether through apps or social media.
- Stalking is an indicator of future serious personal harm (McFarlane et al., 1999).
- Breaching your privacy: accessing your phone/social media, your handbag/wallet or other personal things in your home.
- Asking for loans: may convince you it is a genuine situation and promise to pay you back.
- Mistreating pets/children/your property: animal abuse often precedes police callouts for family violence, and there is a link between pet abuse, child abuse and partner abuse (Campbell, 2022).
- Showing heightened interest in your kids: for single mothers caution is key.

Common excuses used by men who abuse women:

- She winds me up; If you poke the bear of course it will react.
- I'm under so much stress at work.
- She knows I have jealousy issues, but she always flirts with other men.
- It got out of hand because she made fun of me.

- It was just a little tap.
- She just doesn't know when to stop nagging.

Commonalities found in men who abuse women:

- Justify their behavior and twist blame - 'Look What You Made Me Do' (Hill, 2019).
- Minimize their behavior – "That didn't happen – and if it did, it wasn't that bad – and if it was, I didn't mean to do it – and if I did – it's because you made me."
- Gaslighting – "that's not what I said – No way is that what happened – you are lying - why do you have to be so emotional – you really need to go and see a Psychologist – you need help."
- Charismatic – (Jekyll and Hyde), can appear as a really amazing guy in public or social situations but once in private and behind closed doors his character totally changes. e.g.: "You're the one with the problem, even your friends (or kids) like me."
- Don't like the 'no' word – expectation they decide on everything, e.g., "What do you mean you've got a headache and want to stay home, I've already made the plans so we are going to my mate's party whether you like it or not."
- Coercion – a form of black-mail to get you to do what they want, e.g., "You're so frigid, if you aren't going to have sex with me there's plenty of other women out there who will and I won't waste my time on you anymore."
- Cyclical pattern – unhealthy relationships with abusive men often show a to ongoing occurrences of the abusive behavior. This is known as The Cycle of Violence/Abuse (Walker, 1979)

The Cycle of Violence and Abuse:

Any woman who has been in an abusive relationship – (or grew up witnessing one), will recognise that there was a pattern at play in which an explosion would happen where you want to leave but he coaxes you back with promises the abuse will not happen anymore, so you believe him and stay, but eventually it happens again. Sometimes the cycle can play out every week, or it could be a yearly occurrence.

It is extremely important all women understand the cycle of violence and abuse (see diagram below) and the significant role that the absence of personal responsibility plays in allowing it to continue. If you are to find yourself in any situation with a partner who displays any form of abuse - depending on the seriousness and whether it is a deal breaker – if you are utilising assertive communication and setting a clear boundary(we will cover in Chapter 7) that this will not be tolerated if it happens again, you need the strength to take required actions if and or when it happens again. Most abusers do not take personal responsibility for their actions or commit to what is needed to manage their behavior – and as long as a woman fails to take responsibility for her life and safety, this keeps the cycle in play and the abusive behaviors will continue (Walker, 1979).

"Past Behaviors are the biggest indicator of future behaviors."
(Paul Meehl)

"An Apology without changed behavior is just manipulation."
(Sierra Monaee)

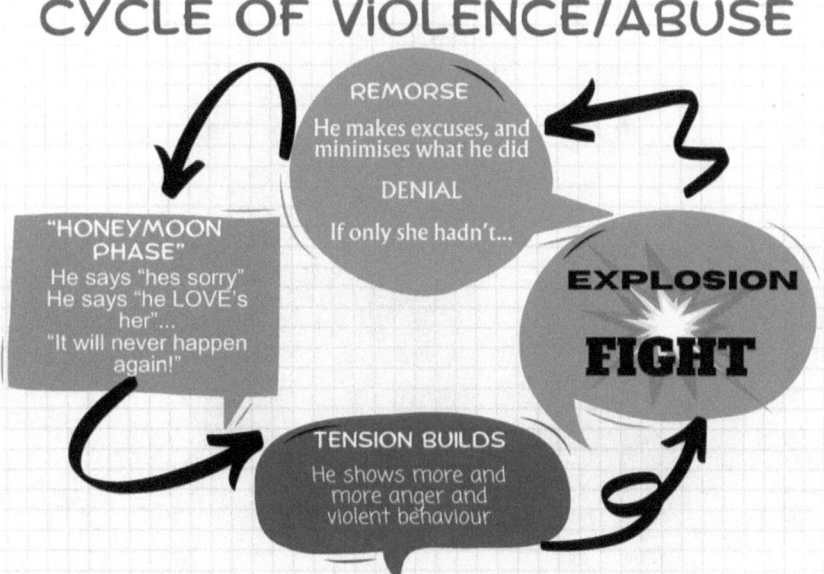

CHAPTER 6

The Path to Healing and Recovery

This Chapter is a guide for any woman who identifies as one of the following and wants to create change in her life: (although will hold relevance to every woman's path of DA - prevention, growth and empowerment).

> Have been in an abusive relationship?
> Caught in the 'cycle' of abusive relationships?
> Witnessed or experienced DA in childhood?
> Currently living with DA? (contact nearest Women's Refuge for support)

RECOVERY from DA and the healing journey requires a commitment to undertaking a combination of activities and practices. In this chapter and following, I am sharing components that were embedded in my *15 Week Trauma Recovery and Empowerment Program-* which is now offered in three separate components (information is in the resource section along with information on a range of other relevant supports). The Journey varies for each of us, as does the time it takes. It is highly important that you place your focus on your growth and learning, and not be distracted by entering new relationships until you have reached your goals. The activities and practices that I am recommending will comprise:

- *Accessing therapies and counselling to address your trauma (possibly support groups).*
- *Creating your personal daily/weekly Self-Care-Plan that incorporates holistic wellbeing(healthy mind, body, spirit).*
- *Re-educating your Self-Talk and Self-Beliefs to overcome negative programming.*
- *Learning how to set boundaries with assertive communication.*
- *Developing personal safety awareness and strategies.*
- *Learning the differences of Healthy Relationships Vs Unhealthy Relationships.*
- *Developing an understanding of your Rights and ability to have them respected.*
- *Finding your place in a network of Compassionate and Empowered Women.*

The Healing & Recovery Journey: (non-linear & overlaps)

[Counselling] + [Learning] + [Changing] + [Self Care] + [Remove] + [Create Your]
[Therapies]   [& Skills]   [Negative]   [& Holistic] [Toxic]   ['Bucket-List ']
[(Inner Child]   [Self Belief] [Well-being] [People &] [& Set Goals]
[Healing)]   [Things]   ['Well-Done']

ALWAYS REMEMBER TO HOLD ON TO THE HOPE THAT YOU TOO WILL GET TO LIVE A SAFE AND HAPPY LIFE
(I know this from my own Journey and the hundreds of Women whose Journeys I have witnessed)

DO THE WORK AND TRUST THE PROCESS

HEALING OUR INNER PAIN AND TRAUMA

Trauma: the Australian Psychology Society defines trauma as, "very frightening or distressing events [that] may result in a psychological wound or injury [and] a difficulty in coping or functioning normally following a particular event or experience." (NCDVT & MH).

A simple definition is "… more emotion than a person can handle…" (Heal for Life, nd) and gets locked in our brains and also parts of our body. When experienced in childhood it actually changes the way the brain develops.

Unresolved trauma in women is linked to many comorbid disorders, and the highest burden of non-fatal illnesses, as well as problems in interpersonal relationships, family and employment (Trevillion et al., 2012); in addition, places them at high risk for entering abusive relationships.

Whether experienced in childhood or at any time in our lives, the effects of being abused creates a vast range of feelings, such as: shock, anger, sadness, betrayal, disgust, disbelief, shame, and more at the inner realization a violation has occurred. Depending on our situations, most times when we have been abused, we have had to continue on in our life's roles and bury the pain inside. In addition, we may not have been able to tell anyone or to get help due to threats, fear and shame – hence we had to keep it secret and receive no support or comfort. Many women have so many layers of pain and hurt shoved inside them, meshed in with the negative messages that are retained in their Inner Self Belief Template, yet still have to function in their daily lives with the responsibilities, expectations and potentially ongoing fears of further abuse.

> Many DA victims say they feel like they are wearing a mask to the outside world because they have to hide the dark-parts and secrets held within. In the Gallery Section you can see a range of masks from survivors that were part of the 'Healing Broken Wings' exhibition I held.

How unhealed trauma can be presenting in your life: many survivors are so used to being a certain way, they do not even realise that unhealed trauma is impacting them in how they behave, think, feel and more. For example:

- Emotional hyper-reactivity: highly sensitive; cry easily; get angry easily; insecure; over-think, etc.
- Chronic people-pleasing: you do everything you can to make other people happy/and like you.
- Get confused and overwhelmed by certain situations.
- Hate criticism: this can present as arrogant when in fact your 'ego' is so fragile.
- Fear rejection and/or being abandoned: (or 'left out').
- Fear of confrontation and avoid asserting yourself.
- Socially isolate yourself and have difficulty making new friends.
- Live on high alert.
- Feelings of mistrust and betrayal.
- Deep feelings of anger and irritability.
- The underlying reason for many mental health problems or addictions.
- Depression and feelings of hopelessness.
- Headaches, stomachaches, chest pain.
- Linked to suicidal ideation (and actual suicides)

Healing:

"Healing is an active and internal process that includes investigating ones attitudes, memories and beliefs with the desire to release all negative patterns that prevent ones full emotional and spiritual recovery" (Myss, 2001).

Accessing therapies and counselling: (including phone or online to achieve the best healing outcomes, I suggest combining counselling and therapies. For ongoing holistic well-being, see more in chapter 8)

Counselling: finding a counsellor you feel comfortable with and who has required qualifications, experience and a back-ground in DA and trauma is of extreme benefit in the beginning of your journey, and for however long you feel necessary. Most counsellors will let you know the approaches they prefer, and what I have heard effective from women I have assisted: (although there are others)

- CBT (Cognitive Behavioral Therapy) -Transactional Analysis -Schema -Narrative -Somatic
- EMDR (Eye Movement Desensitization & Reprocessing)
- ACT (Acceptance & Commitment)
- Dialectic Behavioral Therapy (specifically for Borderline Personality Disorder)

Counselling for those on low income: where financial restrictions have prevented you from seeking Counselling, there are a range of free or low-cost options available. A Health Care Card provides eligibility in Australia to request a Mental Health Care Plan from your GP which provides a set number of discounted sessions from a range of Counsellors.

Free community counselling: certain charity organizations or church-groups offer counselling with persons who may have some level of experience and qualifications, but not registered with the national professional organization (in Australia it is the Australian Counselling Association).

Free phone or online counselling:

- TRAUMA SPECIFIC: Blue Knot Foundation: 1300 657 380
- DA SPECIFIC COUNSELLING: Full Stop Australia: 1800 385 578
- DEPRESSION & ANXIETY SPECIFIC: Beyond Blue: 1300 224 636

Other Forms of therapies:
Hypnotherapy; Art Therapy; Sound Healing; Dance Therapy; Bowen; Kinesiology; Reiki; Barrs; Access Consciousness; Mindfulness; Trauma based Yoga; Inner Child; Mirror-Work.

Learning and skills: a large part of the healing and recovery journey is actually unlearning and letting go of the negative messages and conditioning you have received in your life that are locked in your inner self belief template and replacing with positive and affirming messages and recognizing your rights as a woman. Already in this manual you have acquired a great deal of knowledge regarding DA, as well as uncovering your risk factors and IRPS. You can consider the further learning as a scaffolding of layers of knowledge, and within this section you will learn the steps required to create the solid base that will sit beneath those layers, and which is the essential component of a strong – safe and empowered woman with a high sense of self-worth who sets firm boundaries.

This is broken into 4 parts:

(1) Self-Care and Holistic Well-being (more in chapter 8)
(2) Letting go of the negative messages and thoughts, and creating positive thought patterns (more in chapter 8)
(3) Creating self-worth and self-love (more in chapter 8)
(4) Setting boundaries (covered in next chapter 7)

(1) Self-care and holistic well-being = self-love: depending on your individual life journey, and the situations you have been in, it is highly likely you have given a lot of your energy into others and ensuring their needs were met - for those who are Mothers/Carers this extends even further. For many of you, it is likely you have neglected caring for YOU! which is how we nurture our well-being and also, sends a message to others of how much you value your self – **"We Teach Others How To Treat Us."*(Tony Gaskins)***

"Your body is the temple of your soul," and to honor yourself, you need to care for your mind-body-soul because each aspect is interconnected. This approach is known as Holistic Well-being and is the path to living a healthy, balanced, harmonious and productive life in safety and with healthy relationships (Hays, 1989).

HOLISTIC WELLBEING

PHYSICAL	**+ EMOTIONAL**	**+ SOUL/SPIRIT**
(food, exercise, rest)	(positive thinking, stress management)	(a harmonious and calm life)

As a woman on her Healing Journey you will achieve far enhanced benefits from this approach. The mind-body connection is now well recognised. Women who have trauma from sexual abuse have higher incidences of uterine fibroids, cancers, endometriosis, and other conditions; internalised anger contributes to a range of digestive and gut issues (Hays, 1989). In her book *'A Mind of Your Own: The truth about Depression and how women can heal their bodies to reclaim their lives'* Dr Kelly Brogan & Kristin Laborg explains how dietary, lifestyle and thinking practices creates the best path for recovery from Depression (2016).

> **(2)** a: Letting go of negative messages, thoughts, and emotions
> b: Creating positive thought patterns:
> (Please review the Inner Self Assessment (3a) Chapter 10)

Utilizing your Self Worth Assessment data and the ACES test you did earlier, with your knowledge of what forms of abuse and negative messages you have received in your life, and you will now recognise the level of harmful and unhealthy impacts on your inner template of self-worth which links into the constructs of your sub-conscious mind and your belief-systems. THIS IS IMPORTANT! How we THINK influences how we FEEL about ourselves – which influences what we ACCEPT into our life and our CHOICES. Our sub- conscious mind links to our brain chatter and self-talk and is at work 24/7 feeding us with negative messages, which then flows into our feelings and behavior, as shown in the diagram below:

```
              .....>>.......BELIEF/THOUGHTS......>> (playing in Self-Talk)
BEHAVIOUR/AFFECTS THOUGHTS              FEELINGS/BEHAVIOUR
              <<<<<<<<<<<<<<<<<<<<<<<<<<<
```

By consciously controlling your thoughts and self-talk with positive rather than negative, you then can control your feelings and emotions - this changes your energy – how you interact with people - how they respond to you - increases your happiness hormones - your life enjoyment and your life journey (Engel, 2006)

Example:

Negative -THOUGHT: "It's all hopeless, I was an idiot for being with '...' I'll never

>   FEELING/BEHAVIOR: have a decent boyfriend and I'll always feel miserable. I'm just going to drink away my pain."

Vs

Positive -THOUGHT: "I am doing all the daily activities on my path to healing and

>   FEELING/BEHAVIOR: recovery, every day I feel stronger. I am creating a positive ME and when the time is right, I will meet a decent partner and enjoy a healthy relationship."

It is a proven fact – you can change your thoughts, attitudes and feelings by engaging in a daily program that incorporates a range of practices such as: affirmations, journaling, mirror-work, relaxation, exercise etc. (In Chapter 8 we will look into these more thoroughly, along with strategies for letting go of the negative messaging you have received in the past).

(3) CREATING SELF LOVE AND SELF WORTH

"You just need to love yourself more" they said!! - "HOW" I asked???

Of the hundreds of women I have worked with, low self-love and low self-worth have been the common factor they shared, which I understand because that was me for a large part of my life. I fully believe that creating high self-love and self-worth is one of the most important protective factors in reducing the risk of entering an abusive relationship or staying in one. However, it is almost impossible to develop self-love and self-worth without applying several factors into your life: The 3 C's

> **You need to make the CHOICE to create the CHANGE and CULTIVATE new habits.**

It takes effort to work on your personal development and your healing journey along with changing thought patterns as discussed previously and practicing holistic well-being and self care.

As you continue through this manual you will learn more about developing self-love and self-worth and will find a range of suggestions in the resources. There are so many ways to nurture and care for yourself on this journey as you learn to honour yourself and connect to your inner power, you are building your **PREVENTION TOOL-KIT** to keep you safe from domestic abuse.

POEM: 'AS I BEGAN TO LOVE MYSELF' by Charlie Chaplin.
As I began to love myself, I found that anguish and emotional suffering are only warning signs that I was living against my own truth. Today, I know, this is **'AUTHENTICITY'**.

As I began to love myself, I understood how much it can offend somebody if I try to force my desires on this person, even though I knew the time was not right and the person was not ready for it, and especially because this person was me. Today, I call it **'MATURITY'**.

As I began to love myself, I understood that at any circumstance, I am in the right place at the right time, and everything happens at the exactly right moment. So I could be calm. Today, I call it **'SELF-CONFIDENCE'**.

As I began to love myself, I quit stealing my own time. Today, I only do what brings me joy and happiness, things I love to do and that make my heart cheer, and I do them in my own way and in my own rhythm. Today, I call it **'SIMPLICITY'**.

As I began to love myself, I freed myself of anything that is no good for my health – food, people, things, situations, and everything that drew me down and away from myself. Today, I know this is **'LOVE OF MY SELF'**.

As I began to love myself, I refused to go on living in the past and worrying about the future. Today, I live each day, day by day, and I call it **'FULFILLMENT'**.

As I began to love myself, I recognised that my mind can disturb me and it can make me sick. But as I connected it to my Heart, my mind became a valuable ally. Today I call this **'WISDOM OF THE HEART'**.

CHAPTER 7

Assertiveness Training for Safety & Early Intervention for Our Girls

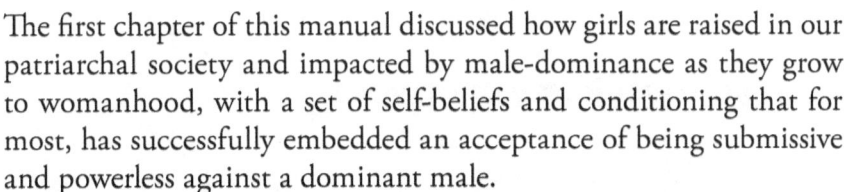

The first chapter of this manual discussed how girls are raised in our patriarchal society and impacted by male-dominance as they grow to womanhood, with a set of self-beliefs and conditioning that for most, has successfully embedded an acceptance of being submissive and powerless against a dominant male.

In my years of working with women, as well as teens and from running the *'Keeping Us Safe'* High School Program, I have recognised the dismal lack of specific assertiveness skills such as boundary setting; assertive communication; red flags and consent awareness (which ties back into the societal conditioning). This set of skills can be termed assertiveness training and early intervention training for prevention of abuse. I cannot over emphasise the astounding changes that occur as a result of gaining this package of information, learning and skills.

To successfully achieve the goal of prevention of domestic abuse and wage the war against gender-based abuse, we need **every woman** armed with this TOOL-KIT, and we must be teaching it to our daughters.

In this Chapter I will be sharing assertiveness training from my Empowerment Self Defence program. Learn this and apply this and you WILL change your life! I will then share a section committed to early intervention training for our daughters, and information directed to how we can raise them to overcome the negative and harmful gender stereotyping. There will be a section graciously provided by Anita Roberts (Founder of *Safeteen Canada*), which is an acclaimed violence prevention program created over 40 years ago and now offered in most schools in Canada. Anita has authored books, is a Tedtalk and Keynote Speaker, and is on the Canadian Federal Task Force on Ending Gender-based Violence.

I am thankful to call Anita a friend and mentor, and it is Safeteen, Ca. that is the foundation of the school program I have provided, and my 'Women's Empowerment Self-Defence Program'. Her immense wisdom and experience will be embedded in the real-life applications that you will be able to transfer into your parenting to help create an empowered young person able to make healthy choices and defend her rights.

ASSERTIVENESS TRAINING

Every aspect of this links into boundary setting, but to set boundaries confidently you need to have developed high levels of self-love, self-value and self-worth. Please refer to Chapter 10 and do the self-assessments: (3a) and (4) to give you a good idea of where your current levels are, plus what your current boundary setting competency is. The more you love, value and respect yourself, the less likely you are to put up with disrespectful behavior and will have a greater ability to communicate your feelings and your expectations from others in a calm and non-threatening way.

BOUNDARIES: whether or not you have experienced abuse in your life, most women rate poorly in their ability to set boundaries and have difficulty saying NO. When we place these aspects in the context of abuse-prevention, it means we need to learn how to communicate very clearly what we like and agree to and what we do not – and if our requests are not treated respectfully we view this as a red flag or deal breaker. This also ties into consent and non-consent – there can be no perhaps, maybes, okays and silences. Once we implement boundary setting through the correct communication style, we are creating the best prevention of abuse strategy.

"Lack of Boundaries Invites Lack of Respect."
(Mousa Coaching)

It takes time and practice to successfully learn these skills, especially if you are a woman who experienced harsh parenting, or have endured abuse already in your life, as you were not able to assert yourself due to fear. Trust that as you keep growing your self-love and self-worth and commit to this path step by step, you too can accomplish this.

We set boundaries in many situations and for many different reasons. A boundary is our way to protect ours (and those we love) territory-possessions-wellbeing: physical, emotional, mental, sexual, spiritual, financial, etc. When we set a boundary, we need to have an awareness that the other person may not be able or willing to change their behavior, and that we need to be ready and prepared to take whatever action that is required in response.
'It is our responsibility to protect & take care of ourselves & what we value.'

'Boundary setting with communication is an essential tool for parents.'

- Setting boundaries is a vital step in taking what control we can of how we allow others to treat us — so NO MORE BLAMING OTHERS FOR HOW THEY MAKE YOU FEEL!!
- Sometimes if we fail to let the other person know their behavior is negatively impacting us and our feelings are being hurt– they actually may not know. By letting them know you are giving them the choice to change their behavior – OR – face the consequence.
- When we understand the role of boundaries, we realize that we are not required to take responsibility for another person's behavior, because it is their responsibility to deal with the consequences of their own choices and what they have-or have not-done.
- Setting boundaries shows our love to our self. It is how we define– *Our NEEDS - OUR FEELINGS – OUR VALUES and BELIEFS* and do what is required to uphold them.

Once we start to have a more loving relationship with ourself and recognise our worth – we start to naturally and normally set healthy boundaries with others, speak our truth, own our rights and let others know how we want to be treated = Healthier Relationships.

EXAMPLE OF SETTING A BOUNDARY

- A situation where you are being spoken to disrespectfully.
- Set a Boundary using calm Assertive Communication (see below)– NO BLAME -
- NO HOSTILITY- NO CONTROLLING- state the CONSEQUENCE if request ignored.
- If you do not get the required response that respects your request – you then need to Follow through with the

Assertiveness Training for Safety & Early Intervention

> CONSEQUENCE – OR – depending on situation you have the CHOICE to walk away.
> - You accept their reaction/response/ issues – as their responsibility – YOU CAN NOT FORCE THEM TO DO WHAT YOU ASKED.

Sometimes setting boundaries is hard work- it takes bravery because when you share your feelings you become vulnerable, raw & exposed (but here is where you gain your inner-strength and build your self-power- pride - authenticity by speaking your truth and making a stand for your rights. You may lose people, but what you gain is self-respect and clarity of a situation or person that is not respecting your needs and values).

Key Points to Remember

IT IS NOT MY JOB TO FIX OTHERS	IT IS OKAY IF OTHERS GET ANGRY	IT IS OKAY TO SAY 'NO' NOBODY HAS TO AGREE WITH ME
IT IS MY JOB TO MAKE ME HAPPY	I DON'T HAVE TO TAKE RESPONSIBILITY FOR THEM	I HAVE A RIGHT TO FEEL MY OWN FEELINGS

Please see the Brené Brown link: https://www.youtube.com/watch?v=TLOoa8UGqxA

ASSERTIVE COMMUNICATION: is how we use our words to set boundaries. It expresses our rights, values, and feelings. It is not an effort to control another person or blame (some may interpret it that way). It is also our way of keeping safe from harm, threats, and abuse. It is a skill set that needs to be practiced until you have learnt it and are confident to use it. Learning these two things well

– boundaries plus assertive communication will create change in every part of your life.

Sadly, less than 5% of the population practices assertive communication and this is seen as a major contributing factor to: relationship breakdown (and abuse); family breakdown; employment problems; illness; loneliness; mental distress and more (Bolton, 1987). The famous psychologist Carl Rodgers stated:

> *"The whole task of Psychotherapy is dealing with a failure in communication.."*

- Learning assertive communication allows you to have healthier connections to people in many ways, you put less energy into self doubt due to fearing the other person didn't understand you; allows you to lose the need for defensiveness and gives you the chance to feel comfortable with your opinions and just being you. You develop self-respect + greater happiness. You can have your needs met and defend your rights and personal space without abusing or dominating another person (how the other reacts is their issue- not yours).

SKILLS NEEDED:

1. Listening skills.
2. Emotional regulation and anger management.
3. Ability to honestly name your feeling resulting from the other behavior.
4. Assertive communication – 3 part message using voice intonation and body language.
5. How to manage Dispute Resolution/Conflict Escalation/Safety Risk.

1. Listening skills: how well we listen will impact our ability to utilise effective, assertive communication. The average person has poor listening skills and absorbs only 25% of what the other person is saying, because they are busy thinking about what they want to say next, or just tuning out(Bolton, 1987). The more we practice really 'listening' so we can fully understand where the other person's intents are, the better we will set boundaries.

2. Emotional regulation and anger management: in Chapter 8 there is extensive information on enhancing our emotional wellbeing and cultivating inner calm. Depending on each person's history and where they are on their healing and self-development journey will directly influence their capacity to manage their emotions and anger, which is necessary to effectively set boundaries. Basic breathing exercises and positive affirmations can be of help.

Successful assertive communication is compromised whilst you or the other person, is angry, or under the influence of alcohol or other drugs. If it is too difficult for you, in some situations you can communicate in written form – however, this will only work if the other party has enough emotional maturity and willingness to respectfully deal with the situation.

3. Name the feeling: in some situations, this is very easy, but in the context of establishing a relationship with someone you have developed feelings for, who is doing something that is hurting your feelings it requires you to be vulnerable and real, with the risk they may object and find a reason to reject you. If you do nothing and pretend everything is okay – you are doing yourself a disservice and not showing self-respect, and potentially aligning yourself with someone who does not have your best interests at heart and putting yourself at risk of abuse. No matter the extent of your vocabulary you know in your heart and your gut when something is not right. Find any words you can to convey the impact – and use it in your 3 part message.

4. 3-Part message: using choosing consequences: vitally important to deliver with a calm voice, relaxed body language, facing the person and with respectful eye contact. You must remain focused on the main issue and not allow yourself to be drawn away. (The exception is a situation where you are setting a boundary for personal protection -see last example).

- [1] **'When you**........ '(be specific, refer only to what the central issue/behavior is… what Has upset you. Non-blaming)

- [2] **'I feel**….' (use feeling descriptive words… be real, honest and true)… **'Because…..'** (Short explanation of the impact of the issue/behavior)

- [3] **'Next time I would prefer if …'** (state what you would like)…. /or **'if you choose to do this again… next time I will…'** (consequence)

Examples:

"You never listen to me. You are constantly interrupting and being rude. You really have no clue how to have a conversation**," VS**….."*When you talk while I'm talking I feel annoyed, because it seems you are not hearing anything I'm saying. Next time we talk can we take turns so you can listen to me and I can listen to you?*"

"Stop yelling at me, you scare me," vs… "*When you are angry and yell at me I feel scared – if You CHOOSE to do this again I am going to leave because I won't be around yelling and anger.*"

"You've got to stop drinking. It is ruining our family," vs.. "*When you choose to get drunk around me and the children, I feel really worried and scared. Next time it happens I will take the children and go stay with my parents. It is your choice to not deal with your drinking and my choice to not be around drunken behavior.*"

(Create some examples relevant to your situation and practice…
practice….practice)

IMPORTANT:

We need to show self-respect by taking honest ownership of our feelings and acceptance that the other person is making their own choices. We can not change them. We cannot force them to be what we want them to be.

The only path forward is to acknowledge our feelings and make our choice of how we will act to ensure our personal safety and wellbeing.

What steps are needed? set boundaries and deliver the consequences.

Not everyone is going to like you or respect your boundaries and that's ok.

Honor your feelings. Certain people may try to twist them, disregard them, make fun of them. Recognise this as abuse and act accordingly.

Example: Setting a boundary for personal protection and safety: in these situations you use strong eye contact; a dead pan unexpressive face; a strong voice to deliver your message and if possible, hold your hand up in front of you in the 'stop' gesture.

Example: you have someone in your personal space and you are feeling violated. You are at a party and a male has moved up close to you and placed his hand on your thigh whilst making crude sexual suggestions. (Remember you have **RIGHTS**)

> *"You are invading my personal space. Remove your hand and move away from me Now! Or I will scream for help."* (or whatever applies to your situation). Do not look away – keep staring directly into his eyes with your hand raised in the 'stop' gesture.

If he does not do what you requested, repeat the boundary once more, if he still does not respect your instruction- follow through with the consequence.

(If you would like to learn more 'Empowerment Self Defence' see the link in resources).

5. How to manage dispute resolution, conflict escalation and safety risk

Disagreements and disputes are a part of our everyday lives and will present in every space where you have relationships, such as with partners, families, friends, workplace and other situations. Without a good application of boundaries and assertive communication based on emotional regulation and self-worth, these disagreements can quickly escalate into hostility and conflict. Successful resolution will depend on whether the other person or persons have these skills also or if they are operating from a place of power and control.

Most women I have worked with over the years share a dread of and avoid confrontation to sort any form of dispute, which is understandable for women who have experienced abuse and harmful anger like yelling and threats. It is also tied to our societal conditioning. When we avoid confrontation, we hold a simmering anger inside of us which harms us physically and mentally. We may eventually explode into conflict, where we cannot control what we say or do, with the potential of saying and doing harmful things we may later regret. Depending on the other person, we put ourselves at a serious risk of harm. As you become a safe and empowered woman, you will develop a greater ability to deal with disputes and make choices that will protect you and keep you safe. This is important for abuse prevention. How a potential or current partner conducts himself in disagreements with you or others is an indicator of either emotional control or risk and danger.

I will present guidelines for managing disagreements and disputes (that will also be relevant to parenting). When you learn and practice these skills from a place of calmness and respect, you will be amazed at the results and the empowerment you will feel.

NOTE: Your Safety is #1. Be aware of the other person's behavior and reactions that can present danger and be prepared for steps you will take if that occurs.

1. Time-outs and disengaging from a power struggle: is a key skill to utilise in any situation where a disagreement is commencing, emotions are heightening, voices are raised. Using assertive communication state you require a time out. You could say, "I'm feeling unsettled at the moment and want to have a timeout so we can both calm down. I'm going to go for a walk and when I get back, I would like it if we can sit down quietly to discuss this issue."

During time outs you take steps to regulate your breathing, calm your emotions and think positive thoughts. Do NOT allow the other person to re-engage you (putting up the stop hand works well) and remove yourself. Once you have calmed down, have a think about the issue and ask yourself, *what choices do I have here – is there room for negotiation?* The answer will determine your next step in deciding is this a dispute resolution situation, which you will communicate further when you both sit down to talk or will you be asserting your stance on this issue (and depending on the situation you implement the appropriate actions).

2. Steps of dispute-resolution and potential consequences: (Bolton, 1987)

- Create an agreed on time to have a quiet talk (need a quiet space and both calm).
- Define the issue.
- Communicate your desire to reach a good outcome.
- Succinctly state your views, needs, feelings on the issue.
- Listen to the other persons, do not interrupt, reflect back to be clear.
- Identify and break down key points.
- Try to work through and to negotiate.
- Reflect your thoughts using "I statements," about what you can and cannot accept.

- Reach the best situation possible- realising either of you will not get what you want.
- If the outcome does not align with your values and wellbeing you need to choose what your steps will be.
- If the other person is using disrespect and threats to control the outcome, this is 'abuse' and you need to choose your next steps.

> As we develop our self-love, self-worth, self-value and are prepared to take required steps to defend our rights, and gain competency in setting boundaries using assertive communication we will approach any situations requiring dispute resolution with a different perspective, and very naturally we will remove from our lives people who pose risk or harm.

Consent understanding: consent is the cornerstone of any respectful relationship in every setting, and ties in with our rights and being respected. When discussing the relevance of consent to the prevention of all forms of gender-based abuse and you look again at the 'Power and Control Wheel' in Chapter 2, it is obvious how a woman loses her right to use consent to have any control over things that happen to her.

Within our development of assertive communication as a means to keep ourselves safe in future relationships and in all settings, women (and girls) need to be fully aware of the need to utilise consent as their way to have control over what they agree to take part in, and what they allow others to do to them.

Consent is especially important to understand in how we navigate relationships and the development of boundaries as intimacy progresses and into when sexual intimacy begins. Without very clear expressions of consent certain sexual acts can occur which the woman really did not want, which then come into the realm of sexual assault and leads into trauma and multiple harmful consequences. "If both partners do

Assertiveness Training for Safety & Early Intervention

not enthusiastically consent to any sexual activity (including kissing and touching) a crime may be committed." (WAAC, 2017). If you are being coerced or blackmailed, with something along the lines of, *"if you don't have sex with me there's plenty others who will,"* this also becomes a criminal act. **Consent = rights!**

Part of consent is learning to say NO – which is not: I'm not sure; maybe; silence or varied other unclear comments. It is also necessary to know that just because you have consented to a particular sexual act, does not immediately mean you have given consent to others; in addition, consent can be withdrawn at any time. Becoming a safe and empowered woman requires you to fully honour your body and your sexuality and know how to use consent to ensure nothing occurs to you that you are not enthusiastically wanting to occur and that you are retaining your personal power.

Red flags: (See Chapter 5). A situation where another person displays disrespect; harm; posing risk or disregarding your requests can be an early indicator for abuse, and called a red flag indicating danger. This awareness is woven into your ability to utilise assertive communication for your safety and the prevention of abuse.

The more you love yourself, the more you will view red flags as deal breakers.

Early intervention for our girls:

'When should Early-Intervention begin? In the Womb!'

As this manual has made clear, the impact of exposure and the experience of domestic abuse and the hardships it brings, have a direct influence on our psychological and emotional susceptibility to becoming victims of abuse. The greatest gifts we can provide our baby in the womb, is for us to be safe. Let them grow with strong attachment; nurturing; love; safety and model themselves upon safe and secure adults with positive, safe relationships. This requires each of us to do what we can to be the best versions of ourselves and put serious consideration into choosing the men we allow to enter our lives to become the fathers of our children and do all we can to avoid being in an abusive relationship.

For every woman reading this manual, who is a mother who has experienced abuse and is negatively impacted by trauma, you cannot change the past – and it does you no good when reading this to feel guilt for what impacts have already been imprinted on your children. The steps you take moving forward to be free from abuse and to heal and empower yourself is a valuable gift by the efforts you are taking to break the cycle of abuse and violence and be a role model in teaching your daughter (and sons) to also be safe and empowered within themselves.

The assertiveness training information applies to our girls also (modified for age). As parents, you need to be teaching from the earliest age possible, along with building up their self-worth and self-love. These should be embedded prior to their teen years. We know that once children reach between 12 – 14 years of age, parental influence decreases, whilst that of their peers increases, along with hormonal changes and the natural development of their sexual identity.

As parents, we can equip our children for the risks they will be exposed to in their everyday lives, e.g. boundary setting; consent awareness; assertiveness; and age appropriate abuse prevention knowledge (*Anita Robert's section will tell you more*). This includes proper naming of body parts for our younger children and awareness of what behaviors are abuse, along with ensuring they have identifiable safe persons who they will tell if any form of abuse or violation occurs.

Boundary setting also applies to us as parents. Whether a single mum or a unified couple, parenting is difficult and becomes more challenging during adolescence. From my personal experience, and the hundreds of mothers I have supported I have witnessed the harsh impact on emotional and mental wellbeing, from trying to maintain influence and control with our teens for their safety and general daily living while dealing with their non-compliance and often rage. The stronger we are within ourselves, the greater our capacity to set the limits required for their guidance and healthy development. Continual attention needs to be paid to our self-care and the varied practices of holistic wellbeing as described in Chapter 8, along with accessing a support network and specific professional support when you recognise either you are not coping or there are serious risks presenting in your daughter's life that you are unable to manage.

I would like to share the following wisdom from Anita Roberts (Founder of Safeteen) and will then provide the core concepts of the Safeteen Program which provide a well-proven foundation in teaching self-awareness and personal safety to our girls (further links will be provided in the resources section Chapter 10).

Anita Roberts: Founder of Safeteen

SAFEKIDS

strong.smart.safe

Strong kids get to stand up. **Smart** kids get to speak up.
Safe kids get to grow up.

"It is never too early to begin giving our children skills to stand up for and protect themselves, which is done by teaching them the difference between reacting from fear or anger, or responding with **Inner Power (assertiveness).** Kids as young as 3 and 4 years old can learn how to do this. Using role-plays is the most effective way of doing this because it creates a body-memory of using the skills. One of the very first skills we can teach our little ones is **the STOP HAND**. Body language is 85% of communication. We can also add simple words such as, **'No'; 'I don't like the way you are talking to me'; and 'Stop, I will tell'** – and emphasizing 'keep no secrets' of anything someone has done to them.

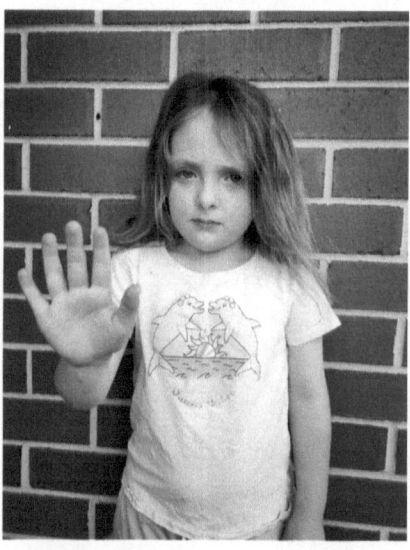

- **How do we make our children strong?** It is crucial to give our children (age appropriate) information about the risks and realities of the world they live in. When we hold back the truth of what's out there we may feel we are protecting their innocence – and in fact we are. However, we are keeping them in a 'happy bubble' which makes them more vulnerable and less prepared in every way. The truth is that this bubble will be popped at some point. The only question is, do we want this moment to happen in a safe and supportive atmosphere, or do we want them to be blind-sided by something abusive, aggressive or shocking that they had no idea was coming, and in a situation where they have no support? How can a child be prepared to stand up for themselves if they don't even know what's out there? **Information is power. Safe kids know how to stand up.**

- **How do we make our children smart? Boundaries:** When we give our children agency over their own physical, verbal and emotional space and especially their own bodies we empower them. By respecting their boundaries and modeling our own healthy boundaries we are teaching them that they have a right to speak up and even prevent violations. These teachings can begin in infancy and can be reinforced through all the stages of childhood and adolescence. If our children do not know where the line is, guaranteed it will be stepped on repeatedly. A child who is unaware of their boundaries is an easy target for all forms of abuse. To offer a child both the permission and the ability to speak up when their boundaries are crossed is true empowerment. When we teach children about personal boundaries, how to identify them, how to assert them and how to protect them, we are giving them a form of intelligence that will serve them their whole lives. **Smart kids know when and how to speak up.**

- **How do we make our children safe? Skills:** Perhaps the most important piece to put in place in order to keep our children safe is to give them actual **hands-on skills** so they can navigate all the confusing, intimidating, painful and potentially threatening moments they may have to deal with every single day. Firstly, we can help children identify situations where they are uncomfortable, afraid and potentially at risk. Secondly, give them a simple and effective skill set that they can apply to any or all of these situations as they come up. Thirdly, offer them a safe environment to embody those skills through role-plays and practice with them how they could navigate those moments in the safest way. We cannot be there to protect our children every single moment of every single day. School age children are alone out there most of the time. What our children need so desperately is a range of strategies that they can access when they are in a high-pressure moment. Children with skills know how to **stand up, speak up and grow up safe**. The **3 Girl Archetypes** and the **Safe House-Dangerous House** are the simple and core foundation of what is taught in the **Safeteen Program** and a summary will be provided at the end of this chapter. Below is information on developing our daughter's **Core Essence** which becomes a powerful tool to keep them safe in all situations, including online.

Teaching Girls Self Esteem and Safety by Developing their Core Essence

Our **core s**elf is the part of us that is at our centre and our core essence is the part that defines who we are- our beliefs; values; individual qualities; interests; skills and more.

How the female core is stolen from us: Our core can be eroded just by being female in a patriarchy, plus external forces such as abuse or violence (experiencing or witnessing) in any form can also erode our core-self, as well as: bullying, gender stereotypes, racism, homophobia, and sexism – the most pervasive and insidious is: **sexual harassment** (proven link to **self-esteem** loss in girls as they progress into adolescence).

Assertiveness Training for Safety & Early Intervention

"If we want to nurture the '**Core-Self**' of our daughters, we will stop telling them how beautiful they **LOOK.** We will begin telling them how beautiful they **ARE**" - Anita Roberts

How to cultivate her core essence: When we feed something it flourishes and grows stronger. We can feed our daughter's **core self** by showing her we value these attributes in a range of ways (see below).

How her core-essence is damaged: If she is not able to stand up for and honor her values and beliefs, and if we - or others harm it in our words and actions. If this happens over time, she will lose it in bits and pieces, and over the months and years, her core self gets smaller and more fragile, which in turn makes her more vulnerable. Another form of damage is the harmful habit of negative self-talk (which is actually internal bullying). A powerful skill to teach our children and youth is to become aware of the things they are saying to themselves, and to practice countering those messages with positive self-talk. In Safeteen we use the metaphor of the '**Mean Fairy**' and '**Kind Fairy**' to demonstrate Negative Vs Positive '**Self-Talk**'.

Says mean things- is a bully and makes us feel Says beautiful and positive things to us that we are useless and no good. tell us we are worthy, clever and good.

Understanding core-essence: our society places a heavy focus on girls to be a certain way - pretty, attractive and sexy – to appeal to the male gaze. Females are given these messages at a very young age that what they look like, what they wear, their hair, eyes and shape and size of their bodies are the most important things about them, and crucial to attracting boys! That is what is noticed and commented on, (or for some girls, not noticed and not commented on). The results of this over and under focus on appearance can be devastating to the core self of the girl-child, as well as having an implicit connection to their vulnerabilities for attracting the wrong attention and exposure to multiple dangers. As parent's we can counter-balance these risks by cultivating their core essence.

Our developing girls need to be receiving positive validation as they are developing their self-identity, so we can choose to focus on their inner qualities and strengths. We can help them see that there are two mirrors. One reflects the surface qualities, and one reflects the core essence of who she is. As we begin to practice reflecting a girl's core essence we are cultivating that same practice inside of her. Ultimately, the goal is to nurture a girl's ability to see herself, from the inside-out. A person who sees and values who they are will be more likely to develop their strengths and qualities as they have self-value which allows them to set boundaries that honor their rights, keep themselves safe, allow them to fulfill their potential as a person regardless of gender or physical appearance.

Core-Essence compliments: do not have a focus on physical appearance which pertains to stereotypical attractiveness, but it could include a physical feature. For instance, to tell your daughter (or a girl) she has beautiful hair/clothing is focusing on the physical attribute **versus** saying you admire the way she does her hair/or chooses her clothing, which is a comment about an internal quality. The quality being praised is her **creativity.** Here are some examples:

- You are so beautiful *to me*.
- I like the way you do your hair.
- Your sense of style is so original. I really like your look.
- I like you so much.
- You're a good friend.
- I respect your clear, strong boundaries.
- One of the things that I like about you is how genuine you are.
- I am impressed with how hard you are willing to work.
- I admire the way you stood up for yourself.
- Your strong spirit is awesome.

Assertiveness Training for Safety & Early Intervention

Remember: deflect and reflect – deflect the question and reflect the inside quality of your girls. Shine the light on their essence

Am I pretty? You are way more than pretty. You are radiant! You are smart and brave and funny and creative and original. I could never fit you into a word as small as pretty.
Am I pretty? You are beautiful to me in every way.
Am I pretty? What do you think? Is it important? What does being pretty mean? Why do you think girls all want to be pretty? Would you rather be pretty like a Barbie doll or unique, creative and powerful like, Taylor Swift and Beyonce?

The Foundation Teachings of Safeteen: safe house versus dangerous house **and 3 Girls.**
(Website links and information regarding resources and programs will be in Chapter 10)

2 Houses: You can do this activity with two pieces of paper and draw the two houses or can do it this way –Imagine in each of my hands (hold up your two hands), I am holding a **hard house** in my Left Hand, and an **easy house** in my right hand. Let's describe the hard house – it has a 10-meter-tall brick wall the whole way around, with barbwire on top and a very high iron gate with pointy tips on the top, which has a big lock and needs a key to open it. There is a big-scary guard dog. All the windows have bars on them and the front and back doors have triple security screens. It also has security cameras right around the whole property.

Let's now describe the easy house – flimsy and pushed over fence, windows open, no security doors and the front door looks like it's been smashed and doesn't shut properly. Imagine there is a really mean burglar prowling the streets and at one end he sees the hard house and at the other end he sees the easy house. Each of these houses has a valuable car in the driveway and he knows the keys will be in the house. Which house do you think he will break into?'

The goal of this exercise is to transfer the concept to our body and what can we do to make our body a hard house to keep it safe, so no one touches or takes from us what is private and precious. You then can conduct role plays using the stop hand and assertive language, (eg. sitting at bus-stop and a creepy guy comes and sits close to you and making sexual comments). This is an exercise in **boundary setting** and **self worth** which we require to keep ourselves safe. It also ties into the next aspect which is the **3 Girls**. Once they understand – do this role-play and get them to act out each of the **3 Girls** and how they would deal with creepy guy, and create other role-play scenarios. Be creative and use real life situations.

POWER GIRL: is really brave, wise and smart and knows how to be calm, even when a bit scared. She knows her rights and speaks her truth.

TOUGH GIRL: is always angry and mean. She gets into fights a lot. She is not very smart, but she is brave and not scared of anyone. She gets in trouble a lot because of her bad temper. She does not want to be called a **nice girl**.

SHY/TINY GIRL: lives in the easy house. She's quiet and shy, always looking at the ground – doesn't make eye-contact, shoulders hunched. Would never tell anyone to go away because she is scared they might get angry with her, and she wants to be a nice girl. So she says nothing, even in situations like the creepy guy sitting next to her at bus-stop, when she is feeling 'icky' and scared inside. **Not speaking her truth.**

By discussing these three girls and the hard and easy house you create the opportunity to explain how we need to learn not to be shy, tiny girl or to be an easy house and that we want to be power girls and hard houses. Also, that in some situations we need to call on the tough girl if someone is violating our boundaries and attempting to harm or force us to do something and we need to get away from them and be tough and strong because being the nice girl will not keep them safe. These are amazing safety lessons. Role-plays, that when done with one girl or a group of girls, can be fun whilst teaching these valuable lessons, which are early intervention abuse prevention.

> "Teaching our children how to make choices from a place of inner wisdom is the best prevention strategy of all," by Anita Roberts.

CHAPTER 8

Living as a Safe and Empowered Woman

One of the goals of this manual is for the reader to live as a safe and empowered woman, and possibly inspire or play a role in assisting other women to do so also. In this chapter I share significant characteristics and practices that need to be developed to become a safe and empowered woman and expand on holistic wellbeing as the self-care that maintains your body, mind and souls and is essential to achieving this goal.

CHARACTERISTICS OF A SAFE AND EMPOWERED WOMAN

- Recognises she is responsible for her feelings and well-being, she gives no one else control, holds high emotional maturity.
- Has high levels of self-love; self-worth; self-esteem; self-value and self-confidence.
- Has healthy emotional regulation; self-calming and anger-management practices.
- Practices good self-care using holistic wellbeing for her mind, body and soul.
- Knows her rights and actively pursues and protects them.
- Not afraid to speak her truth, even knowing others may not agree or approve.
- Communicates her needs and feelings using assertive communication.
- Sets boundaries and follows through with consequences.
- Recognises red-flags in people and situations and takes necessary actions for safety.
- Calls-out discriminatory and sexist behavior she sees in others.
- Values and strives for harmony, peace and balance in her life.
- Is happy and fulfilled as a single woman 'Alone not Lonely' or in a 'Healthy Relationship'.
- If in a relationship or planning to be in one, has high standards and will not settle for less.

1) A commitment to personal development: for women who have experienced abuse, continuation of your healing and recovery journey. For every woman, a commitment to the practices required to build self-esteem and self-worth. Cultivate a recognition of inner self qualities and the unique aspects you hold that create the essence of who you are.

2) A commitment to personal safety: keeping an awareness of the categories of abusive men, red flags, utilising boundaries and assertive communication to protect yourself and your rights. (see end of this Chapter).

3) Personal responsibility and power: when you learn your feelings are your responsibility and have gained the skills to control them, you gain personal power. This means you will no longer blame others, e.g., 'You make me so angry', therefore, now and in the future, no one has power or control over you. This is a BIG-STEP on your journey. For women who have experienced abuse, it also means you have learnt to let go of any anger and resentment toward those who could control and harm you in the past. In addition, learning to manage your sensitivity and emotional reactions through acceptance and detachment frees you from expending energy into trying to change others, instead you can just focus on your safety, inner wellbeing, and personal peace.

4) Maintaining emotional well-being: accessing support where required and practicing self-care to allow for emotional regulation, stress and anxiety management and calm dispute resolution skills. For women who have experienced abuse this is another BIG-STEP.

5) Good self-care and practicing holistic well-being: (body/mind/soul-spirit): The combination of these practices creates balanced well-being; high self-love; positive thinking and demonstrates to others the value you place on your self and your worth. (You may like to take the How Good Is Your Self Care Practice questionnaire (6) in Chapter 10).

> "With every act of self-care, your authentic self gets stronger, and the critical, fearful mind gets weaker. Every act of self-care is a powerful declaration: I am on my side, I am on my side, each day I am more and more on my own side" (by Susan Weiss Berry).

BODY: diet; hydration; exercise; sleep; plus attention to any ailments and accessing therapies to keep your body healthy and in balance (also to heal trauma).

MIND: emotional/mental health and positive thinking practices: A combination of self-care practices to keep yourself okay. Ensuring you seek professional assistance if you notice you are struggling and for those with trauma to continue on your path of treatment and therapies. Maintaining a positive and stress-free mind-set can be achieved through the following:

Daily positive affirmations: an affirmation is a selection of words that you say for a set number of repetitions, which if done consistently will create new neural pathways and new positive self-beliefs which builds self-esteem and can assist in self-calming, e.g., I am calm, centered and balanced. (more provided in Resources).
Mirror-work: saying positive messages to yourself whilst looking in the mirror.
Letting go practices: there are a range of activities known to be effective: writing down the negative messages you have received and then burning them, combined with a release mantra (Engel, 2006); and certain therapies such as reiki which works to remove negative energy you are holding in parts of your body.
Practicing daily gratitude: when you are thinking thoughts of gratitude, it is impossible for your brain to process a negative thought. Take time each day to think or say out loud, things you are grateful for in your life.
A sanctuary in your mind: close your eyes and create your special-safe-sanctuary, fill it with beautiful things. When you feel agitated or worried close your eyes, take some deep breaths in and out and imagine yourself there for as long as you need/are able, or use in your meditations.
Meditations: a daily practice is recommended in which you either have a special spot in your home, or in nature, and either seated or laying down, close your eyes and focus on your breathing, whilst pushing out all other thoughts (varied forms available).

Self-calming & mindfulness: get to know your body and be aware of the changes-signs when you are getting stressed/agitated. When you recognise your body stress signs, try to have some quiet time and do some self soothing strategies: deep breathing exercises; go to your imaginary sanctuary; gentle music. Another strategy to use if you feel yourself getting angry in a conversation, practice and pause –before responding. This allows you to take a breath and think up something to say that will not inflame the situation, and demonstrates your self-control.

Avoid taking things to heart: recognising your inner-peace need not be disturbed by petty things that are said/or happen. Accepting other people's dramas belong to them, not you. When you choose not to instantly react and instead just let it go or use humor you are practicing self-control by not allowing the other person to press your buttons and control your emotions.

Connections: having a sense of belonging and purpose is important. Depending on your personal interests, there are many community-groups available plus volunteering opportunities. Contact your local council or library to get information and contacts.

Music: calming meditation music can accompany your meditation practice, or can be used at any time as background while you do other activities. Chanting mantras is known as Kirtan or Devotional Singing and is another relaxing source combining gentle music with rhythmic affirmations, e.g. *I Am The Light Of My Sou'* by Ajeet Kaur.

You can seek out local Kirtan-Circles and be part of the pure energy that is shared.

Read: positive uplifting books: (see in 'Resources')

Time in nature: or other outdoor activities: Proven to enhance our wellbeing.

Apps: Happify, Headspace.

Avoiding negativity: Staying away from toxic people, situations, music, movies, etc.

Self-Love: all of these above practices contribute to raising self-love, along-with setting boundaries; ensuring you are treated with respect; and caring for your soul.

Soul/spirit: can be a religious practice, or a way of being and thinking that believes your soul and spirit is connected to a higher universal source of goodness, love and light.

Many practices help you reach deep relaxation; happiness; and inner peace which flows back into giving benefits to your mind and body, and link also into a range of therapies which also promote healing benefits for those with a history of trauma. Developing your awareness and connection to your divine feminine essence.

Therapies beneficial to your MIND/BODY/SOUL-SPIRIT: Crystal Bowl Sound Healing; Tai Chi; Qi-Gong; Yoga; Meditation; Chakra Clearing; Crystal Therapy; Bush-Flower Remedies; Homeopathy; Theta Healing; Tantra; Reiki; Bowen; Acupuncture; Art-Therapy; Time in Nature; Drumming; Journaling and more.

6) Set goals for your future and bucket-lists: "The majority of DA survivors I have worked with struggle to create a timeline of where they are now, and then with markers 3 months, 6 months, 12 months, 2 years and so on. An empowered woman has faith and trust in herself, and realises there are no barriers for her to set goals for her future. Positive thinking practices and efforts aligned will support your goals and are the path to creating your future. A goal is a dream with a date on it." (Proctor)

In addition, you can create a bucket list of treats and adventures that you can work towards to celebrate your achievements or to create special memories with your children, family or friends, "If you can believe it – you can achieve it." (Proctor).

> It is so rewarding for me seeing ladies who completed my Recovery Program over the past years, who are now living the most amazing lives and accomplishing great achievements. I can recall for every one of them our first meeting, and how sad

> and broken they were, with no hope for their futures. (Some will be shared in Chapter 12).

7) Being a voice for women's rights, gender equality and ending GBV: every one of you can play a role, whether by supporting public figures or organizations that are platforms to highlight the call for action (unwomenaust.org.au) or joining groups who advocate for women across the globe, e.g. Plan International (plan.org.au) – or by being the one to phone the police if you see a woman in danger of abuse, or quietly passing a Women's DV Service card to a woman in your community who you suspect is experiencing abuse.

*"**Feminism** has fought no wars. It has killed no opponents. It has set up no concentration- camps, starved no enemies, practiced no cruelties. Its battles have been for education, for the vote, for better working conditions, for safety in the streets, for childcare, for social welfare, for rape crisis centres, women's refuges, reforms in the law. If someone says, 'Oh, I'm not a feminist', I ask, 'Why, What's your problem?'"*
      (Dale Spender, Man Made Language).

WOMEN'S RIGHTS: are the fundamental human rights that were enshrined by the United Nations for every human being on the planet nearly 70 years ago. Every safe and empowered woman knows these rights – is not afraid to fight for them for herself or for another woman. The more safe and empowered women who achieve this, the closer we move to reducing the gap of gender inequality and the prevalence of gender-based abuse, which is the principal goal of this manual. The full details of the Declaration of Human Rights can be found in the Resource Section.

PHYSICAL:
I HAVE A RIGHT TO —
- be free from physical violence
- decide who can touch me and how
- my own personal space
- make my own decisions about my body
- make my own decisions about my physical appearance
- access healthcare of my choice
- safe accommodation and access to necessities, e.g. food and water

SEXUAL:
I HAVE A RIGHT TO -
- be free from sexual violence
- say NO to sex or any sexual activity that makes me uncomfortable
- insist on safe sex
- change my mind about having sex

EMOTIONAL/PSYCHOLOGICAL:
I HAVE A RIGHT TO -
- say no to things asked of me
- be treated with respect
- be free from verbal abuse and all forms of emotional/mental abuse
- have my own opinions and beliefs
- express my feelings
- make my own decisions and pursue my interests
- privacy and freedom
- prioritize my self-care in the way I choose

SOCIAL:
I HAVE A RIGHT TO - -see friends and family
-engage in social activities and make new friends
-work or study
-access support networks if and when I choose
-have fun

FINANCIAL:
I HAVE A RIGHT TO - -choose how I spend my money or save it
-choose to earn an income

SPIRITUAL:
I HAVE A RIGHT TO - -choose and practice my own religious or spiritual beliefs

CHAPTER 9

'Are You Ready To Date'? and 'What Does A Healthy Relationship Look Like'?

The focus of this manual has been on raising awareness of DA and providing paths of self-development towards becoming a safe and empowered woman, with minimal risk of connecting with an abusive partner if and when you believe you are ready to consider dating or seeking a life-partner. Regardless of your dating and relationship past, if you are a woman ready to date this chapter provides helpful reference information to enhance optimum outcomes along with checklist of recommendations you should pay attention to prior to, and then in the early stages, that could be what saves you from ending up in a harmful situation.

"Make sure you feel good about yourself before you ask someone else to feel good about you." (Brecht, 1997)

DATING AND RELATIONSHIP READY: whether you are a woman who has been on her healing and recovery journey to overcome previous abuse related trauma, and or a woman who has or has not been in previous abusive relationships, making the choice to date requires you to feel confident you now possess high levels of self-worth and self-value and have the qualities described in the previous chapter of a safe and empowered woman. If this is not the case, you hold great potential of attracting a partner with characteristics that were described in Chapter 5. For a 'Woman Who Loves Too Much,' commencing dating before complete recovery, can be likened to a former alcoholic attending an open-bar-party and thinking, *just a couple of drinks will be fine.* (Norwood, 2008).

You need to think about entering into a relationship as you would think about buying a house; or car; or business! Your most precious asset is your life so before investing your life and your future to be merged with another person's, why wouldn't you approach with caution, do your homework by researching into everything about this person so you can feel as confident as possible that your future will be safe and secure. In this early period of time it is extremely important to rule with your head and not your heart so that if you uncover red flags and deal breakers, you are in a position to extricate yourself with minimal risk of harm. It may cause you some tears, but what a small price compared to many years of suffering and pain from finding yourself in an abusive relationship (Brecht, 1997).

Dating and Relationship Ready and Coping with Rejection: as a safe and empowered woman you will be aware that you have opened yourself to the potential of connecting with someone who seems a great person and you commence dating but then find yourself rejected. This is where your emotional maturity will deal with the situation differently in comparison to the woman you were with low self-esteem to whom this could have had many negative impacts. This is another self-check in because if you recognise this person has just done you a favour and was obviously not worth your time and effort, you can be assured you have progressed. If however, this triggers hurtful emotional thoughts that will be connected to your past it is a sign you still have more healing to do and it is not the right time to be dating.

> "Rejection – and the fear of rejection is the biggest impediment we face to choosing Ourselves." (James Altucher).

Broccoli Vs Chocolate Cake: you also need to be aware of any patterns you have of attracting a certain type in the past. This is particularly important for those of you who realize your exes had a 'Bad Boy' element that you were drawn to, which ultimately ended up creating chaos and pain to your life. In her book *'Women Who Love Too Much'* Robyn Norwood explains this as being a common factor for those who have been raised in dysfunctional homes with the *'highs & lows'* of chaos, and that by choosing dangerous men you are keeping in the zone of what actually feels normal to you and that sub-consciously you may have felt that was all you were worthy of anyway.

As a Safe and Empowered Woman you are now creating a new-normal by looking at the good qualities and values you wrote on your list of what you are seeking in a partner, you can view this as relationship broccoli that will give you what you really need in your life versus relationship chocolate cake that ultimately was the unhealthy choice that ended in sadness and pain. When you commence dating broccoli, it may feel strange initially, however keep reminding yourself of your new path and your goals for your life and your future.

Falling in Love: as part of our societal feminine conditioning, we have been infiltrated by so many distorted-romantic beliefs about the process of dating - finding a partner - and falling in love. As safe and empowered woman we need to play a much more active process in deciding on a person, starting with creating a *what qualities and values am I looking for* list, and ensuring you do not settle for less. Also, take things as slowly as you want. It is okay to stay in the good friend zone for as long as you require and give yourself time to get to know this person, do the checks, and see how they act with differing people and in differing situations. By not investing too much emotionally too soon – you are protecting yourself.

Are you being pressured: there is great societal pressure which can be added to from family members or friends – trying to tell you that you need to be in a relationship. The phrase "being left on the shelf", or even worse, being called "a spinster" was in times gone by deemed as personal failings of a woman. As a safe and empowered woman, you are the one choosing your future path and need not comply with any-one else's views or expectations.

Intimacy: once you have taken the step and have created a connection with someone you are attracted to, it may be difficult to refrain whilst in the getting to know him stage – but becoming sexually intimate will most likely result in you forming a deeper emotional connection and losing your ability to be objective if red flags appear. Also, depending on your previous IRPS you may have actually used being sexy and provocative as a strategy to keep a man interested in you (Norwood, 2008).

There is a saying, "Men give Love to get Sex and Women give Sex to get Love,"- if by chance this has applied to you in the past, taking this different approach is likely to feel strange and challenging – by sticking with it you will be showing your progress and will allow you the time to learn more of this person. Many of the dangerous characteristics described in chapter 5 can be hidden initially, which is why taking things slowly and cautiously is the safe path to proceed on. If the person you are dating does not respect your choice and commences using guilt or coercion, this is an immediate red flag.

Healthy relationships: to have a happy, loving, and healthy relationship that will carry you through your life is something most of us grow up wishing for – and even for women who have been through unhappy and abusive relationships, it is still natural that most still hold hope they will achieve this goal. Keeping in mind that for many of us we have not experienced what a healthy relationship actually is, from our childhoods and carrying on into adult relationships, it may be difficult to perceive how it works or what it feels like. Following is a checklist of considerations starting from before you commence dating, and then many of the attributes that are found between couples in a healthy relationship.

Checklist for Healthy Relationships:
Prior to dating:
1) Each person holds high emotional maturity; self-love and self-worth; and has overcome any faulty Inner Relationship Personality Style (from Chapter 4); have confident boundary and communication skills, and are both ready to enter into a committed relationship. *(I recommend you re-do the self-worth questionnaire (3a) in Chapter 10 and there is also a emotional-maturity (5) test).*
2) Each person has a clear understanding of the qualities and values they are seeking in a partner. Making a check-list is a good idea: stable job; healthy lifestyle; hobbies; interests; good manners; respectful; kind; has a circle of friends who show similar values as you; comes from a stable family; a person who is committed to self- improvement.

Once dating:
1) Have the important things to know conversations (answers could be red flags or deal breakers). This will be discussed further shortly.
2) Develop relationship guidelines, boundaries and expectations from the beginning (if either/or both of you have children from previous relationships these need to have specific inclusion and will be discussed further shortly).
3) Respectful and honest communication.
4) Able to have disagreements respectfully, fair fighting and things that are 100% off-limits.
5) Spend regular quality alone time where it is just the two of you.
6) Both spend regular time apart (friends, hobbies, sport, etc.)
7) Each shows respect to the other's friends and family, and equal time spent with each.

8) Respectful boundaries agreement regarding social media.
9) Know each other's backgrounds if there is a past of trauma and awareness of relevant sensitivities.
10) Regular self-checking on how you are feeling and any concerns you need to seriously consider, (whether they be regarding him, or you slipping back into prior unhealthy patterns). Remember early intervention and detection of problems, and if necessary politely declining any further dating is the path to your safety and protection from DA.
11) Ask yourself:
   - *Is this connection for the betterment of me and my children?*
   - *Is this connection enhancing my/our lives, now and future?*

CHARACTERISTICS OF HEALTHY RELATIONSHIPS:

- Respectful: sensitive to your feelings and needs; allows you to feel safe and secure in his company.
- Supportive: listens and understands; values your opinions; celebrates your wins; supports your goals.
- Trustworthy: follows through with promises; treats you and your possessions well.
- Emotional honesty: he shares his feelings; you feel safe enough to share your feelings; you are able to be your true authentic self.
- Communication: listens without interrupting or judgement; you feel you are heard; can have disagreements without fear and able to reach agreeable outcomes.
- Sexual respect: respect your boundaries; accepts that no means no; mutual respect to each other's needs and satisfaction; enjoy sacred intimacy.
- Equal effort: in all aspects and in particular in ensuring the relationship is flowing well.

- Economic equality: you create fair arrangements; you have freedom in your choices.
- Enjoy each other: you both are genuinely happy and relaxed together.
- Express affection: shows this in lots of ways.

Important things to know conversations:
Ensure you already know things such as previous relationships; criminal convictions; any major debts; serious health conditions; previous addictions; major family problems; and more.

Other topics: home ownership ideas; re-location ideas; study plans; early retirement plans, and more.
Do we both want children? If there is a mismatch here, it is a deal-breaker.
If both say no, some discussions about the type of futures you are envisioning, e.g., travel or business, etc.
If both yes, many aspects to raise and discuss openly to find out what each of you think on subjects such as number of children and expectations of how long you should work to and when to return to work; the involvement of dad e.g. He plans on only working part-time and being home more to allow you to work; discipline styles; involvements of each person's extended family; type of schooling, and more.

Shared Parenting: either/or both have children from previous relationship and are co-parenting: There are many important and serious considerations that you both need to feel comfortable with, varying accordingly with the gender and age of the children which influences how willingly they will try to adapt to the changes presented. Blended families require high levels of communication, patience and clear guide-lines around discipline and coping in situations where the influences of toxic exes and possible custody battles create stress and negativity.

I strongly recommend seeking some professional assistance from a Parenting Organization. I can personally recommend 'Relationship-Australia' and also their Step-Parenting 8 Week Program.

CHAPTER 10

Assessments and Questionnaires

#1: Adverse Childhood Experiences (ACES) – From your birth and through primary school:
   (Questions based on the (ACE) Study by Felitti et al. 1998)

a) Did your parent or other adult in your home often swear at you/ insult you / humiliate you/ yell angrily / or act in a way that made you feel sad and emotionally harmed? No____ Yes____

b) Did your parent or other adult in your home often physically harm you, eg: push / grab / slap / throw something at you /or 'other'? No____ Yes____

c) Did you at any times witness your parents or other adults in your home fighting, eg: yelling / swearing / physical aggression / property damage? No____ Yes____

d) Did an adult or person at least 5 years older than you ever have body contact with you that was of a sexual nature? No____ Yes____

e) Did you often feel unloved or uncared for? No____ Yes____

f) Did you often experience neglect, eg: nothing to eat / had to wear dirty clothes / didn't have necessary items for school / home alone / unmet medical needs? No____ Yes____

g) Did you wish your home was better, eg: cleaner/ uncluttered / more room? No____ Yes____

h) Were you often told there was not enough money to buy necessary items? No____ Yes____

i) Were your parents separated or divorced? No____ Yes____

j) Did you live with anyone who was a heavy drinker or drug user? No____ Yes____

k) Did a household member suffer mental illness? No____ Yes____

l) Did anyone in your household have involvement with the Police? No____ Yes____

m) Did you feel unsafe and unprotected in your neighborhood? No____ Yes____

n) Did you feel unsafe and unprotected in your school? No____ Yes____

(The greater number of 'Yes' answers, increases the challenges to your early development and will impact all elements of your emotional and psychological profile as an adult)

#2: Were you Emotionally Abused or Smothered as a Child (Engel, 2006)

1. Were either of your parents overly critical of you?......

2. Was it impossible to please your parents, no matter what you did?......

3. Did you get told you were bad, stupid, insulted?......

4. Did either belittle you, make fun of you, make you the object of sadistic jokes?......

5. Did either of your parents give you very little attention, ignored you?......

6. Did either 'over-protect you', make a fuss if anything happened to you, and stop you doing things other kids were for fear of anything happening to you?.......

7. Were you isolated, prevented from having any kid's over, or going to other kid's houses?......

8. Were either very possessive of you, or get jealous if you paid attention to anyone else?......

9. Did either treat you as a friend and tell you their personal problems, or lean on you for emotional support when they were upset?......

If you answered 'yes' to any of the questions from 1 through to 5, you were emotionally abused-neglected. If you answered 'yes' to any of the questions from 6 through to 9 you suffered from emotional smothering or emotional incest.

#3(a): Your 'Inner-Self' (Self Love; Self Value; Self Worth; Self Esteem)

Rate yourself out of '10': '0' is lowest '10' is highest

What rating is your level of loving yourself………

How do you rate your happiness …….

How do you rate your-self as an 'empowered woman' ….....

Answer 'Yes' or 'No'

Do you ever have deep feelings of not good enough? ……..

Do you find it hard to express your feelings to others who are hurting you? ………….

Do you sometimes have anxiety about your future? ……………

Do you sometimes wish your life was different? ………….

Do you hold deep feelings of sadness deep inside you can't talk to anyone about? ………..

(If you scored between: 21 – 30 your self-worth is doing great, 15 – 21 needs improving, and beneath 15 lots of work is needed to improve. If you answered just one 'Yes' answer, there are avenues in this manual to follow to overcome what is impacting you negatively.

#3(b): Reviewing Negative Influence on your Self Identity / Self Love

Tick LOW / MEDIUM / HIGH	LOW	MEDIUM	HIGH
1) Aspects from baby years through child-hood			
2) Aspects from your school years			
3) Aspects from teen to young adult years			
4) Aspects from relationships – partners			
5) Aspects from sexual interactions			
6) Aspects from work/study places			
7) Aspects of adult family relationships			
8) Aspects of motherhood (if applicable)			
9) Aspects of sexual harassment			
10) Aspects of sexual abuse			
11) Aspects of your health and any treatments			
12) Aspects of societal influences/pressures			
13) "other" – please specify			

#4: How Are Boundaries Working In Your Life

When we set a boundary we are letting the other person know how we feel about something they do that is affecting us negatively, what we would prefer, or a consequence if they do it again.

Rate yourself out of 10: 0 is lowest, 10 is highest

-How do you rate yourself setting boundaries with:- Friends…………
-Workplace/ or place of study …………………………………………
-Family …………………………………………………………………
-With partner or former partner ………………………………………
-Strangers, eg: bad drivers, people pushing in front of you …………
-How do you rate your ability to calmly express your emotions…………
-How well do you get your needs met when you communicate them …………………………………………………………………………..

-In general, how do you feel you manage explaining to someone that something they are doing is upsetting to you/hurting you etc……. …………………………………………………………………………

-How good are you at saying NO when someone asks you to do something, or help them out, when you really do not want to …………………………………………………………………………

-Do you ever say YES to doing something because you are 'afraid' what might happen if you say NO? …………………………………………… …………………………………………………………………………

-Do you ever feel certain people take advantage of you? ……………..
-Do you avoid confrontation? ……………………………………………

-How good are you at dealing with situations when someone sets a boundary with you? (e.g. do you get defensive, or angry, or do you accept graciously?)……………………………………………………..

-From doing this questionnaire, do you feel you need some help with boundaries? ……………………………………………………………

#5: Emotional Maturity and Self-Control Test (Brecht, 1997)

Emotional maturity is measured by your ability to remain calm, positively focused and solution-oriented no matter what is happening in your life.

Answer the following statements by choosing the one which is most like you and then writing in the number:
Very much like me ...3, somewhat like me...2
Maybe, maybe not...1 no, not at all like me ...0

- When I get angry, I can get myself back under control..........
- I am responsible for the times when I get moody and irritable ....
- I am aware of and can control my anxieties, fears and panic ....
- When things overwhelm me I can get my act together quickly ......
- I generally say what I am thinking when needed and do not bottle things inside me .....
- I am responsible for my own feelings, others cannot upset me unless I allow them to .....
- I feel good about who I am and what I can achieve in my life .....
- I believe I am certainly important to look after and do nice things for .....
- I do not let others criticisms of me affect me for too long .....
- If I feel down or anxious I know I can get over it by being positive and solution focused .....

(Tally up the numbers) Your score and profile:
    30 – 25: You have a very healthy level of emotional maturity.
    24 – 15: Borderline. Sometimes you may be ok and other times not. More work needed,
    14 – 0: This score indicates you need support and need to do more work on overcoming your personal struggles. Do not be disheartened please follow the practices in this manual.

#6: How is your Self-Care Practice?

In the 3 categories, tick the ones you do regularly and then review where you are lacking ticks. Put thought into how you can incorporate varied options to ensure each section is being woven into your life for your holistic well-being and self-love.

-PHYSICAL WELL-BEING:

...... Diet: that you eat regularly and food that is healthy for you

...... Exercise: aim for something every-day and set goals to achieve more or try new, and have fun, eg: dance; yoga; Zumba; water aerobics; nature-walks; canoeing, and more…

...... Respect your bodies limits – be mindful of what your body can and cannot do.

...... Good Hygiene: to care for all parts of your body and pamper yourself

...... Medical care and rest when needed

...... Get enough sleep

-EMOTIONAL/MENTAL WELL-BEING:

...... Relaxation and quiet time, eg: meditation; reading; time in nature, and more

...... Join a support group or seek professional help if you have past trauma or specific health issues

...... Access therapies to benefit your emotional balance

...... Decrease stress in your life as much as possible, seek help when needed

...... Set boundaries where needed

...... Make time away from phones and computers

...... Seek avenues for personal development and enhancing emotional growth

...... Maintain connections with friends/family/community

...... Allow yourself to express your feelings and needs

...... Allow yourself to let your inner child out to play and have fun

...... Practice daily affirmations (positive statements you say repeatedly)

-SPIRITUAL WELL-BEING

...... If you have a faith/religion maintain the practices and connections

...... Identify what has deep meaning to you and bring more of it into your life

...... Open yourself to learning about the many ways people spirituality into their lives, e.g.: Meditation; into their lives, e.g., Meditation Yoga; Mindfulness; Kirtan Circles (singing and chanting mantras), and more

...... Commit to quiet reflection time daily, can be in nature or in a special space in your home where you create an alter and have meaningful objects on it, or journal.

CHAPTER 11

Resources

*HOLISTIC HEALTH AND WELLBEING:

-PHYSICAL
- *Edenic Health Body Balancing* – E Health Assessment and Personalized Wellness Plan (https://www.edenichealth.online)

*BOOKS:
- *Heal Your Body* by Louise L. Hay
- *The Body is the Barometer of the Soul* by Annette Noontil
- *Kitchen Pharmacy* by Rose Elliot & Carlo De Paoli
- *The Family Guide to Alternative Health Care* by Professor Patrick Pietroni
- *A Mind Of Your Own: The truth about depression and how women can heal their bodies to reclaim their lives* by K. Brogan & K. Laborg

-EMOTIONAL-SPIRITUAL

*BOOKS:
- *Living in the Light* by Shakti Gawain
- *The Highly Sensitive Person* by Elaine Aaron
- *The Way of the Heart*: Tantra Empowerment for Women and Connecting With Your Soul by Catherine Wood
- *7 Steps to Spiritual Succes'* by Deepak Chopra

*MUSIC, CHANTING, MEDITATION:
- *I Am The Light of my Soul* by Ajeet Kaur (YouTube)
- *Mul Mantra* by Snatam Kaur (YouTube)
- *Gayatri Mantra* by Deya Dova (YouTube)
- *I Am Woman* by Helen Reddy (YouTube)
- *I Am Woman* by Emmy Meli (YouTube)
- *You Are Beautiful* by Cyndi Lauper (YouTube)
- *Roar* by Katy Perry (YouTube)
- *Fight Song* by Rachel Platten (YouTube)
- *I AM* Morning Affirmations for Women (YouTube)
- Varied Meditations and Meditation Music (YouTube)

*PROGRAMS:
- *Daily Om* (www.dailyom.com) A range of online programs
- *The Sanctuary of Ananda* (www.sanctuaryofananda.com) in West Australia (Certified Tantra; Reiki Training; Couples Retreats and Women's Workshops; Books and Resources)

*FACEBOOK:
- *Archaeology for the Woman's Soul*
- *Sacred Dreams*
- *SHE On The Tip Of Her Tongue*
- *The Soul Journey with Sarah Moussa*
- *Sacred Divine Feminine*
- *The Spiritual Mind*

-HEALING and RECOVERY:

*BOOKS:
- *Women Who Love Too Much* by Robyn Norwood
- *The Call To Courage* by Brene Brown
- *Healing The Child Within* by Charles L. Whitfield
- *Healing my Emotional Self* by Beverley Engel
- *Embracing Ourselves* by Hal & Sidra Stone
- *Heal For Life* by Liz Mullinar
- *The Body Keeps The Score* by Bessel van der Kolk

*TED-TALKS:
- Anita Roberts Founder of *Safeteen*, Canada
- Liz Mullinar Founder of *Heal for Life*
- Brene Brown *The Power of Vulnerability*

*PROGRAMS:
- *I Am Woman Empowerment* (www.iamwomanempowerment) (Self Love; Empowerment Self-Defence; Understanding Anger)
- *Heal For Life* (www.healforlife.com) (hold Residential Retreats in New South Wales; Counselling & Groups)
- *Blue Knot Foundation* (www.blueknotfoundation.com) (hold Professional training and a 24 Hour Phone support line)

*FACEBOOK:
- I Am Woman Empowerment Programs- Healing World
- The Mother Wound, by Bethany Webster - Heal For Life
- Co-Dependency, by Darlene Lancer - Freedom From Narcissistic Abuse

*AFFIRMATIONS: (you can find many on-line and on YouTube. These are my favourites)
- I AM CALM, CENTERED AND BALANCED
- I AM WORTHY
- I AM STRONG, I WILL GET THROUGH THIS
- I AM ENOUGH

- I AM FREE TO BE MYSELF
- ALWAYS AND IN ALL WAYS I PROSPER
- I AM OPEN AND RECEPTIVE TO THE GOODNESS AND ABUNDANCE OF THE UNIVERSE
- I PROGRESS MY PATH WITH PASSION AND PURPOSE

*RELEASE & LETTING GO RITUAL MANTRA:
- I RELEASE AND LET GO OF ALL THAT WEIGHS ME DOWN
- I ASK FOR CLOSURE ON ALL THAT IS UNRESOLVED
- I ASK FOR PEACE AND LOVE IN MY HEART
- I AM READY TO LET GO: I AM READY TO MOVE ON
- I WELCOME IN THE NEW – THANK YOU; THANK YOU; THANK YOU

*SUPPORTING AND KEEPING OUR GIRLS/YOUNG WOMEN SAFE: (+ some for boys also)

-BOOKS:
- *Raising Girls* by Gisela Prouschoff
- *Raising Boys* by Steve Biddulph
- *What's Happening To Our Girls?* by Maggie Hamilton
- *Girlhood* by Maggie Dent
- *Safe Teen* by Anita Roberts

-PROGRAMS:
- *Safeteen* (www.safeteen.ca)- based in Canada
    (Has a range of age category school programs for the prevention of violence, some are available on-line; a range of resources; Ted-talk by Anita Roberts; and the Safeteen Book).
- *Safe4Kids* (www.safe4kids.com.au) – based in Western Australia
    (Provides child abuse prevention and body safety programs in schools; professional training; a range of resources; podcasts and children's books).
- *Arabella Hille* – Overcoming childhood shame: nurturing hope, resilience and confidence in children. Ebook and audiobook (https://promotingselfesteem.com)
    (https://victoriousparenting.com)

- *Hush Education* – (www.husheducation.com.au) – based in NSW Australia.
Provides body safety, adolescent and sexual health programs in schools and community programs.
- *Maggie Dent* – (www.maggiedent.com) – based in Western Australia Educator, author and community presentations for parents and schools

FACEBOOK:
- *Safeteen*
- *Safe4kids*
- *Keeping Us Safe*
- *HUSHeducation*
- *Arabella Hille*
- *Maggie Dent*
- *The Man Cave (for boys)*
- *Officer Gomez (online safety)*

****

*BEING PART OF THE FIGHT FOR GENDER EQUALITY

ORGANIZATIONS
United Nations https://www.unaa.org.au/get-involved/
PLAN International https://www.plan.org.au/
https://zonta.org/
https://whiteribbonalliance.org/

The United Nations Declaration of Human Rights
https://www.ohchr.org/en/universal-declaration-of-human-rights

CHAPTER 12

Stories of Hope and Inspiration

'I thank the Ladies whose stories I am sharing'

Karissa's story

Karissa's parents split up when she was five years old and she was forced to live with her mother. The trauma from being separated from her father was then compounded when Karissa's mother entered a new relationship – with a man who would then go on to sexually abuse Karissa until she was thirteen. In her early teens, Karissa was attacked by a stranger who tried to abduct her, further adding to her trauma. Two years after this assault, Karissa escaped from the abusive environment and returned to the care of her father.

At this point, life was good. But, like many victims of childhood sexual abuse, Karissa began engaging in risk taking behaviors, and then entered relationships with men who were physically, emotionally, and financially abusive. During this time, Karissa mothered two children.

After this Karissa entered what she describes as a good relationship with a supportive man and had a third child, but this did not last.

The next man that came into Karissa life, was extremely violent and a drug dealer and in a short time she found herself addicted to methamphetamines. "He nearly killed me," Karissa states. Recognising the danger and her inability to provide for her three young children, she made the decision to hand the children's care over to their father. Karissa stayed in this on and off relationship for 18 months but now admits it was the drugs that kept her going back.

By now, Karissa's relationship with her father had gone downhill. She was staying in a rental property he owned, and he evicted her. From there she spent months living in her car, until her most recent ex-partner smashed all the car windows and slashed the tyres.

Around this time Karissa found she was pregnant with her fourth child. "After my car was destroyed, I had all my possessions in storage but I couldn't afford the payment so lost everything. I was six months pregnant, sitting in a park with nothing and no-one, and rang a crisis hotline that led me to a place in a women's refuge. They gave me support to get away from the violent ex-partner and the drugs. I was able to save money to fly interstate to stay with a relative who wanted to give me support in the final months of my pregnancy." Karissa's daughter was born with a congenital heart condition, requiring surgery at 17 days old. Karissa holds a lot of guilt around her drug use during pregnancy, but this did not impede her desire to find a path to be able to give a good life for ALL her children.

Karissa returned to WA with her new baby and only a suitcase, determined to create a better life. Once she was settled and financially secure, she regained custody of her other 3 children. Karissa had done some counselling but knew that she still had a lot of healing to do – this is when she heard about the 'Safe Woman Safe Family Recovery & Empowerment Program' (SWSF) being provided by Tanya.

Karissa's words: "When I came to SWSF I was still quite unsure where my life was headed and had a lot of unresolved trauma and guilt. I felt scared, confused, and unworthy. My motivation was and always has been my kids. I wanted to break the cycle that I had grown up with, show them that anything is possible if you do the work. I wanted to heal, to trust again, to learn what I needed to do to move forward and to love and forgive myself. I got that and so much more. This Program changed my life and I'm forever grateful.

I healed from past trauma, and became more aware of my own trauma response patterns and behaviors. I learnt how to communicate with men in a much healthier way; I gained self-worth and confidence; I gained knowledge of my childhood and how it had impacted me, and I learnt to let go of thoughts and feelings that had held me back for so long."

UPDATE March 2024: "So many magnificent changes and accomplishments for me since stepping foot into the 'SWSF Recovery and Empowerment program'! **I am a whole new woman**! My confidence is back, I enjoy being social and I am no longer sheltering myself from the world. My anxiety is almost non-existent these days and when it does decide to trick me into thinking something terrible is going to happen, I have the coping skills to pull myself out of that moment. I've immersed myself into some beautiful holistic communities and been blessed with a whole new tribe of supportive and non- judgmental friends. A few of my biggest accomplishments to date would be roughly 5 years ago I set my heart on helping others, I saw an advertisement of a new Women's Refuge opening up and it had a timeframe of 12 months. I put pedal to the metal and started studying hard, (which was actually huge for me as I struggled at school). I passed numerous courses with flying colors and scored myself an interview with the Refuge I'd set my sights on. Low and behold I got offered a permanent part-time position as a Refuge Advocate and have been with the company for almost 3 and a half years!

I then decided to put a little more pressure on myself, and created a new goal of building my own home. I got a second job and sure enough with a lot of hard work, patience and determination I secured some land and am halfway through building my brand new home!! I've successfully set myself and my children's futures up and couldn't be happier. I must also add I became a Nanna in amongst all that! My children are now 21, 18, 9 and 12 and together we have never looked back. Forever grateful xxx"

Georgia's Journey (written March 2024)

I thought once I escaped my abuser, recovery would just happen. I had done the hard part so why did I feel worse?

I came across Tanya's '15 Week Domestic Violence Recovery and Empowerment Program' by chance, I actually rang her because I was looking for emergency accommodation as our abuser found where we were staying, and caused damage to property, plus physical and emotional abuse to my children and I. She told me about the program, and that the next round was starting the next day if I wanted to join. I remember on that first day, we all wrote letters to ourselves and I will never forget in that moment the overwhelming feeling of energy I felt in the room and I knew that this was it, this was where I needed to be and I was going to put everything I had into it. I was going to take control of my life, and give myself and my two young children the life we deserved. I feared my children would be motherless if I didn't.

Our escape happened June 2020, when we were removed from our family home by police with less than 5 minutes to pack our belongings. My Ex – the children's father – our abuser was being restrained at the front of our property /family home. Looking back it was a terrifying and traumatic experience. We were escorted to a refuge and in that moment I made a vow to myself and my children that we were never going back to him, I have stood by that to this day, there were times when I thought my only choice was to return, I sought help from every community resource I could to make sure that didn't happen. This thankfully led me to Tanya.

The first refuge we were placed in was communal living, I was robbed by other women, I was refused extra help as they considered me to have too much money (by this statement they were referring to me having a mortgage on a property I was forced out of to remain safe). In my eyes that made me more financially unstable.

From there, we were taken in by a single mum and her teenage boy. I was still being physically and emotionally abused as I didn't have the courage or strength to say no to the demands I was getting from him still, and the relentless demands to return home.

Over the next two years there was a period where myself and the children were living back in the family home, and he was staying elsewhere – however, he 'broke in' through the roof or window countless times, terrifying and traumatizing situations when the police would be called again. From there I made the moving forward plan. We moved into a safe house provided by an organisation. We shared this with another mother and her children who obviously also had escaped Domestic Violence. I gained legal help and with help from friends, emptied and cleaned the house & got it ready for sale. I didn't give in to his demands and threats around settlement. It sold – settlement went through fairly – and I now have financial security.

Me and my babies are in such a great situation now. Life is safe and stable and we are living in a good house- **Just us!** (no more refuges and shared homes) - they go to a wonderful school, I have bought us a caravan for holidaying and making amazing memories with them that will last a lifetime. I have full custody of the children and he is out of our life. I have just recently started studying my 'Certificate 4 in Community Care' and know I have so much to give in the future helping other women who are going through these struggles.

I lost 10 years of my life married to my abuser. In these last 4 years, with all I have learnt to strengthen myself and all the healing I have done, I've managed to reach a point in my life that when I smile, I smile with my whole body, I feel that smile, that smile shines through me. It's a feeling I never thought I would have. I have suffered mental health problems almost my whole life, along with Type 1 Diabetes- that made my *Healing and Strengthening Journey* just that little bit harder, but also that much more special!

I formed a strong friendship with Tanya, and she has been a great mentor for me. I know I can go to her for any help I may need, her story has been an inspiration and her knowledge is endless. I can say wholeheartedly that she saved me that day I picked up the phone and made that call.

Lynette's Story: 'UNLOVED' (written in October 2021)

My story begins with little love...left alone to cry...no warmth of a mother's love...scared and forgotten...I just longed to be warm, safe, loved and wanted...A family came to look at me...I was cuddled and felt safe...I WAS ADOPTED! As days went by...there was a lot of laughter...lots of people came to visit...looking, touching and holding me...lots of kisses...I wasn't used to so much attention so I smiled a lot!

When I was home alone with my ADOPTED mum, she would very rarely pick me up or give me a cuddle...I had to keep myself amused...I felt LONELY and UNLOVED. When I was a toddler, I would get into trouble...mum would say: 'DON'T TOUCH THAT! DON'T DO THAT! WHY CAN'T YOU BE A GOOD GIRL???? I was smacked a lot, and spent time in my room waiting for my dad to come home. My dad was a bit of a softy, and instead of punishing me would give me cuddles, and ask me to try and be a 'Good Girl' so not to make mum angry. Dad told me many times that MUM LOVED ME...ha ha ha. I found that her love was not the kind of love that I needed or wanted. She was nasty, and I don't know why she ever wanted me. My adopted brother was 10 years older than me and couldn't do anything wrong. He used to pick on me, set me up. He never got punished but I FUCKEN DID! The little love I had was turning into HATE. He moved out when I was 10 years old, leaving me stuck at home with mum alone. Her health was not good, she had diabetes, and was sick and in bed a lot, I had to be quiet, could never have friends over, and she would always tell me, "children are meant to be seen and not heard."

My teenage years were not great, I was sent to an all-girls school – I HATED IT!! I didn't do very well and got into trouble a lot, then I got braces, which made me more of a target for bullying. I left in year 11 and got a job in a Record-Bar and started going out with boys and getting into more trouble! Not long after this mum died. I fell pregnant and had a termination. In that time I ran amok and partied a lot, I then met my husband and we travelled over East. In this time we had a lot of fun, lots of partying and a lot of drugs.

We came back to WA and settled down and had two beautiful children, they were my world. But my husband was changing. He was becoming a violent man, my son had ADHD and my husband would physically punish him. I made the decision to leave my abusive marriage and take my children somewhere safe. It was tough. My son's ADHD behavior was off the rails. He was now hurting me and his sister. This went on for some years. I persevered and got help, I have always been there for them and we got by. They have turned into strong beautiful adults and I am so proud of them.

Sometime down the track, I was settled in my own house with my daughter still living with me, and my husband had nowhere to live, so I said he could share my house! WELL, things were okay for a while until he started drinking again, becoming abusive with me… name calling, putting me down, nasty. Things were bad again. (He still shares my house -but things have changed as I have changed and learnt how to be stronger and set boundaries!).

I walked through the doors of Safe Woman Safe Family (SWSF) 2.5 years ago…I joined the First - '15 Week Trauma and Recovery Program' which was amazing…I learnt to let go of the hurt and regret that I carried in my heart. I learnt about red flags, assertive behaviours, boundaries, communication, and these skills have totally changed my life. I am now in control of it. After the program I became a 'Volunteer-Peer Support Mentor' and have taken many courses to boost my skills and continued all the 'Self-Care practices' to continue my healing. I Co-facilitate the 'Djembe Drumming circle' which is my passion and have assisted Tanya with the '15 Week Program'. I love being part of supporting women and seeing them start off – just like I was - broken, lonely and with no self-confidence, and watching them bloom into strong and vibrant women, and the bonds of friendship that grow.

Follow-up March 2024: Looking back my life has changed so dramatically these past few years. I have worked hard on myself and healing the trauma of my childhood and adult life. My heart is very full – I have a beautiful little grand-daughter, another one on the way and my daughter's wedding. I'm so thankful that I have stuck to my 'Healing and Empowerment Journey' – there have been ups and downs and tears – but I have continued using all the strategies I have been taught. Thankyou Tanya for your advice, help and friendship…. I love my life as an 'Empowered Woman'. To all the Women out there struggling from Abuse & Trauma - **STAY STRONG ON YOUR JOURNEYS – THERE IS HOPE FOR YOU JUST AS THERE WAS FOR ME!**

A MOTHER DEALING WITH 'AVITH' (Adolescent Violence in the Home):

(This Testimonial was provided for the Research Report I conducted in 2018 which can be found at www.iamwomanempowerment.com in the 'Resources' section)

My name is Dianne and my son and I have been going through a terrible situation for the past 5 years. My son was always the quiet, reserved type of child, always studious and gentle natured and a target for bullies. He was picked on relentlessly for being quiet by both students and teachers. Schools would simply dismiss the events and tell me that 'boys will be boys' and that he needed to 'suck it up and toughen up'. Relentless is the only word to best describe the years of bullying at different schools - and it has changed our lives forever.

In the past 5 years, he has gone from attending school every day to only 2 weeks this current year. Last year was about 15%, the year before 40% and so forth as you go back the last 5 years.

My once quiet and good natured boy has turned into a violent, extremely disobedient, spiteful and terrifying young man. He has destroyed property within my home, damaged my car, is repeatedly violent to me - breaking my arm on one occasion - and is essentially my '12 year old abusive husband'. He constantly abuses me, and yet makes calls to the police accusing me of abusing him, laughing as he hangs up and threatens me saying 'I know all I have to do is lie and you will go to jail'. This did result in DCP investigating me this year for Child Abuse! Just last month he 'self-harmed' and then rang my mother to 'Rescue Him'. I cannot even begin to describe the degree of manipulation and terrifying environment I live in every single day.

We have had years of intervention with doctors, psychologists and therapy services, such as DCP, Kids Psychology, MST for 6 months, Police, Down South Therapy, CAMHS assessment, school psychologists, counsellors and Peel Youth Services (who is our current help), I have tried every suggestion but nothing has worked!. My son ignores the therapist or psychologist and refuses to participate - which means people simply give up on us. Tanya – the 'Family Support Worker' has been fantastic in understanding this predicament and has tried with the school and other linkages to get help. Unfortunately there are very limited services and help available to assist us in this nightmare of a situation that we are living. Won't someone please help us?!!!!

I have had to give up work to become a full time carer as my son does not like to leave the house and does not attend school regularly enough for me to maintain employment. Our financial situation is dire to say the least and we struggle day to day to make ends meet. I cannot leave the house, which makes us both essentially prisoners in these four walls. My son is now 12 years old and if things keep going as they are, I fear so much for his future -with no schooling and no socialization, he will never be able to find employment or become a decent, contributing member of society. He will become one of those drop-out, forgotten individuals with failure in their future - which is a tragedy considering he is highly intelligent and a gifted computer programmer. I fear for my future too. I cannot continue to support him into his 20s and 30s. I cannot accept this kind of life is going to be for the rest of our lives.

Follow-up: I am pleased to say that the last contact I had with Dianne many things had improved in their lives. They were both happy and well and he was attending school.

Jen's Story: (written March 2024)

Here is a brief description of how serendipity led me to find Tanya, and subsequently learn how to love and value myself again.

At the age of 51, timelines and dates blurred, my 7th long-term abusive relationship since my first boyfriend at 17yrs (this time 4yrs) came to a sudden, traumatic end. All the verbal abuse, physical abuse to a lesser extent I had endured, the public humiliations, the lies, cheating, betrayals on every level and all the blame placed on me due to my own inadequacies and craziness. It was all flipped around one morning when I defied him. He called the police to have me physically removed from the house. Unbeknownst to me, he had told the police I was the bully, and he was afraid I was going to murder him during the night. I was treated like the abuser. I had 15 mins to collect what I could, not allowed in the kitchen because of knives, before I was manhandled yet again (the police's fingers left bruises on my arms), removed from the premises and given a 12hr restraining order. When questioned, I frantically told them that they had been duped, that I was the one being abused, the male officer just shrugged and said, 'if that's the true case, then why did you stay for so long?' We all know that it is only those who have never been mistreated that would ever ask this question.

I was told I had 2 days to remove all my household of furniture/appliances/heaps of heavy plant pots etc. I was in shock, I had no money and no means to accomplish this – and had to move back to my mother's house. In desperation, I rang the Shire Offices, who directed me to 'Tanya Langford' at 'Safe Women Safe Family'. Somehow she connected with another organization called 'Halo' who somehow had a truck arranged in the required time frame. As soon as what could be moved was, I organised to go in and actually face-to-face meet Tanya. I barely remember the state I was in, that same day when Tanya greeted me at the front door of SWSF. I was in shock, dazed, confused, shamed, humiliated, depleted to a mere shell of myself and completely detached, withdrawn and broken. I was physically ill, with a massive pustular abscess on my upper gum that made the right side of my face swollen. As soon as I spoke, I was listened to my feelings were acknowledged. I was told that I was not crazy. I broke down in tears. It was such a relief. I had been put down and shut down for too long. I was embraced and accepted just the way I am. But I felt this last episode had really broken me and I needed help.

Over the next several months, I got counselling and Art Therapy at SWSF from another incredible woman 'Tracey' who has helped my healing so much. Tanya enrolled me into the '15 Week Trauma Recovery and Empowerment Program' and continued to mentor me. Over this time I worked on not just my grief from this last relationship, but other trauma I had accumulated over the years, which started at school. I had been bullied, nay terrorized throughout my schooling life, with my first fist fight in year 4 and my last at the end of year 10. I also received regular abusive and threatening letters and phone calls. Consequently, I developed a low self-esteem and struggled with bulimia from 14-20yrs. I have been bullied by women in every workplace throughout my life. And on top of the series of bad relationships, I was also attacked one night at my local pub at the age of 45 by friends of my ex's who glassed me in the head...two staples, two weeks of concussion and no CT footage to press charges.

I found a special place at SWSF – made friends and a support network. I became the volunteer gardener there and took great pride in ensuring this environment looked its best. I can say how life-changing it has been what I learnt in the Recovery Program. It delivers all the essential tools for anyone to deal with the continual challenges, changes and daily dilemmas of life with aplomb and self-care, especially when it comes to parenting. And beyond, it is literally a ticket out of hell... for all those who have experienced or are still drowning the depths of humanity. If you are currently or ever been stuck in that deep, narrow pit with any gleam of light obscured from the weight of confusion... if, like me, you have a cycle of insidiously abusive relationships with narcissists who suck the life out of you and you end up alone, traumatized, with nothing and having to start from scratch again, personally and financially...and you want to change your life for the better and break that cycle of mistreatment...then Tanya's program of Trauma Recovery and Self-Assertiveness will literally save your life.

A lot has happened to me in the two years since I did the program. I am now 56yo, the full time carer for my mother with dementia. My brother has been in hospital for the last 6 months with alcohol-related early onset severe dementia at 57 and a brain tumor and now requires 24/7 care. I have taken over all his affairs. I also have serious parenting issues with my young adult children in their early 20s. I am coping with all this by myself, because of the tools I developed. Of course, it is not easy and I have many moments of despair and I still make plenty mistakes. But now I know how my trauma brain works, how to recognise red flags; how to set boundaries; how to communicate, not escalate things when you're triggered, even knowing when you have been triggered, starting to lose your temper and when to just walk away. The affirmations really work, but the greatest lessons for me was to trust my gut, my innate sense of right from wrong. Secondly, to learn not to take on undue responsibility. We can only control what is inside our own realm...that does not include the behaviors or attitudes of others. No, with these we set consistent boundaries as required. Thirdly, no matter how dire and it feels too much to bear... always know that it doesn't stay that way for long, it always gets better as sure as the sun rises and sets each day. We will endure.

I gained commonsense coping mechanism for all the yucky things that happen in life- no matter what life throws at me; I find small blessings and joy in the every day; and I always see the 'silver lining' on every grey cloud and know in my heart of hearts there are good people 'up there' somewhere looking out for me and everything will turn out the best for everyone in the long term.

Thank you, Tanya, for giving me my life and soul back, giving me the tools to keep it alive and the ability to finally put me first so that I can do what I need to to look after all the people in my life to the best of my ability. It gives me such hope that this largely untapped resource of your knowledge will be shared in the Manual you are creating, and can now be found mainstream. I personally believe that this resource should be recognised as an essential component in every life-skills course & embedded within the educational curriculum of every school in Australia. This is positive holistic teaching that everyone should be exposed to. This is how strongly I believe from experience of the benefits of Tanya's program. The success is only limited by your own commitment to follow the recommended steps.

The learnings contained in this book are an untapped resource that will guide your healing and recovery and change your life for the better.

ONE WOMAN'S EPIC-WILL TO DO THE 'RECOVERY and EMPOWERMENT PROGRAM'
(Narrated by Tanya with permission, March 2024)

I met Jacinta when she visited my Information Stand at a Woman's Festival. She was very curious about my 'Recovery and Empowerment Program' and told me about the parts of her childhood she recognised were still impacting her emotional well-being and growth. I learnt she had 2 young boys (still breast-feeding the youngest), and she was also worried about aspects of her relationship with their father.

I told her that I would be starting the next round of the program in a few weeks. Jacinta was determined to enroll and participate. The problem was that where she lived was approximately a five hour drive away from the women's centre from where I was running the program at that time – which consisted of a weekly four hour session for fifteen weeks, plus a weekend live-in retreat. We exchanged contact details, and she said she would call me over next few days once she had talked with her partner, and try work out the HOW!

Jacinta rang me the next day after the festival to tell me she had it all worked out! Her friend who lived on a property near the Women's Centre, had agreed to let her set up a tent for her and the boys to camp there for the 15 week duration, and her friend would care for the boys when she attended. 'It will be an adventure,' she said! (*I still can recall how 'blown-away' I was at that moment – recognising the immense sacrifice this young Mum was prepared to make to access assistance and support for her 'Healing and Empowerment Journey'*). In Jacinta's words 'If you really want to 'change' and break the 'cycles' – and are willing to do what's needed – then anything is possible'.

I knew I had to find a way for Jacinta to have this opportunity without needing to leave home. Even though at that time I wasn't set-up for external participants, I discussed with her the plan I created. This involved Jacinta to do a phone-video link each session – my phone would be in the middle of our table, so all the other ladies got to say hello – and she was able to participate in discussions (I emailed notes prior to each session). It was all a bit hectic; my notes were often hand-written and the phone reception would cut out at times, but WE DID IT!! Jacinta was able to attend one session, and she made it to 'The Weekend Retreat', so we all made wonderful connections with her and she brought a special element to the Group.

I know Jacinta advanced within herself during the program, and she shared with me how different she felt at the end. I also know she worked hard on her self-care practice as well. It has been fantastic following her journey these past few years and know she is a safe strong and empowered woman carving her unique path in life and raising two fabulous boys.

Michelle's Journey (Introduction narrated by Tanya with permission)

When Michelle first rang me enquiring to do the 'Recovery and Empowerment Program' she cried during the whole conversation – and for a big part of the program, she cried. Michelle was 51 and dealing with an ugly property-settlement and child-custody battle from her second long term relationship – which like her first had been abusive. She had three older children from her first marriage, and two younger children (from second) who she only had in her care six nights a fortnight – remainder they lived with their father, and in her words *'they are manipulated and lied to by him'*. Michelle's anxiety and depression was obvious, as was the heavy pain in her heart she was carrying. Michelle did progress during the Program, and it was at our Weekend Retreat she disclosed she had struggled with an eating disorder since she was a child, due to emotional abuse. Once the program was completed, I linked her with a family lawyer I knew, and she navigated the property settlement and also moved to begin a new life.

Follow-up #1: a year after program: 'Letting you know I'm enjoying my life here in…. it's the best thing I could've done moving here! Away from all the gossip, bullying and threats! I have my daughter with me and we have settled in really well. My boyfriend and I are still enjoying each other so much and I have a cleaning job at a motel –it's a family business and the owners are lovely. I've joined the local ladies darts club and am making new friends. My ex-partner and I went to Family Court last week to sort out the property- settlement the outcome was great! I faced up to him, and am pleased and relieved to say he no longer has any power over me, I'm not scared of him! These days I feel like I've healed enough to move on and be the strong, confident woman I was meant to be and used to be. I feel a lot of my success and progress can be attributed to you, your support, advice and friendship. Thankyou x'

Follow-up #2: (2024) 3 years after program: 'I thought I'd let you know that I'm still doing well and wanted to tell you this – I still do my positive affirmations, and sometimes try to look in the mirror and say them, but they always make me cry. But just now I looked in the mirror and said *I fucking love you, you're doing amazing and everything is going to be ok. And I didn't cry!*

It's a huge step for me. And it wouldn't have happened without all the acceptance, help and support you gave me, and for what I gained in the '15 week Trauma Recovery Program'.

These days I'm still with the same beautiful and kind man, I have my own house, and I am working in Aged-Care as a cleaner and also studying/doing a traineeship to become a carer. I love my job and my life. I guarantee your input and influence still helps reframe the way I think.

I have changed so much. I'm confident in myself. The people I meet are kind to me and enjoy me. I feel like I deserve just as much happiness as everyone else. My relationship with my boyfriend is healthy and lovely. My kids are loyal to me and each other and they are all doing so much better. I'm their role model and they want to be each other's role models too. We are all striving to be better and make better choices. I would not have thought this could happen to me –Honestly- It's amazing and also very Empowering. At times it has been tough, but I know that I am here because I have strength, stamina and sheer determination, and also the seeds that were planted when I took part in your Program. I will never forget what you did for me. X'

CHAPTER 13

Gallery – Poetry, Art and Photos

I give thanks to all the women who have shared.

Within Me – by Marney

Well two steps forward, one step back
That's how the journey goes
And exactly just how far I've come I guess no one knows.
Healing is no easy thing
I have to take my time
I can't go pretending
That everything is fine
I spent years at war with myself
I thought it would never end
I took time to find out who I am and now I'm my best friend.
So much time was wasted
Thinking I was always wrong

Now I'm confident within
I know that I am strong
The warrior within me
Let's out her battle cry
I am a force to be reckoned with, No one can deny.

THE OTHER ME – by Marney

There were times in my life
That I never thought I'd heal
I've got scars on my body
From the times I couldn't deal

Had some crazy shit happen
Didn't know what to do
But somehow, the other me
Always got me through
There were so many times
When I didn't know who to trust
When my hopes and dreams

Had all faded into dust
But the me that came before me
Survived; for she was strong
Much stronger than I realized
I now know that I was wrong.
I hated her for the longest time
And I locked her away
But it's because of all she sacrificed
I'm the me I am today

TAKING THE LEAP – by Georgia

My life is being consumed by this and
I wonder if anyone can see the cell I am locked in?
Fear and uncertainty are weighing me down
so much that I cannot breathe
Anger and despair are taking over my body and I've nowhere to go
Shame, regret, rage and then finally comes pain
I shut down in order to survive, I shed no more tears,
I know they do not help
I defy all fear and gravity, I grasp onto this last
feeling of hope so tightly
I have no idea where I am going, nor do I know what this hope is
that I'm following
My heart is racing, I know this is my only chance at survival – a
gamble of life and death
I take the deepest breath
I close my eyes and I leap into the unknown.....
I leapt into **FREEDOM!**

ECHOES OF MY SOUL – by Carolyn

As I dress myself in the morning light,
Lies roll up my body, insight!
My soul echoes feelings of remorse,
the façade covers my true course
Knowing energy remembering my essence, I acknowledge my souls
request with presence
Yet I continue on the bus of deception,
mind control reaching out in all directions
Echoes of my soul, lives past, lived now speaking to the wind
Another leaf falls, haunting voices of A Capella nature
Fluctuating 5D reality, whirling within the matrix structure
Breaking down totality
The Trees keep calling, come, come dear ones
From branches within, more leaves ready for falling

As we drift off each night, Light Being Warriors connect
Meeting ourselves, unite, learning lessons, protect
Connected as one, New earth has begun
Separation no more, Raise up everyone
Destruction personified, Evolution inevitable
Souls come, Souls go, Echoes linger

WOUNDED - by Tracey

I lay huddled naked in a corner
Tears stained my face
Scared to move
For fear of waking you.
Cold, vulnerable and alone
My body ached
My mind shattered
Fragments of myself I waited…
A flower, A kiss, A smile.
Seduced by loving whispers
I fell for you again.
Broken promises…
I was left for dead.
Fear and shame will silence
My voice, and when I
Awakened to my truth,
I realised, I am free.

MY FUTURE HOME

My future home will be a home with no loud anger, no explosive rage,
No slamming doors or breaking glass,
No name calling, shaming or blackmail.
My future home will be gentle, it will be warm, it will keep my loved ones safe.
No fear, no hurt, and no worries.

I may come from a broken and twisted place,
But I will build something whole and safe.
I'll sing in the shower again, cook with a smile,
play my music loud and dance in every room.
I will be '**Me**' again, **Healed and Safe and Strong.**

PUT IT SOMEWHERE ELSE:

You gotta resurrect the deep pain within you
To give it a place to live that's not within your body.
Let it live in Art, Let it live in Writing, Let it live in Music,
Let it be devoured by building brighter connections.
Your body is not a coffin for pain to be buried in,
Put it somewhere else.

HER TASTES:

Her taste in people changed once she started loving her Self.
She stopped wondering if she is good enough for them,
She started wondering if they're good enough for her.

WHAT IF:

What if, instead of expecting yourself to toughen up,
and develop thicker skin,
You created boundaries that honor your softness and sensitivity?

TAKE THAT STEP

Sometimes the smallest step
in the right direction,
ends up being the biggest step of your life.
Tip toe if you must,
But take that step!

THE WOMAN IN THE MIRROR by Donna Ashworth

There's a woman in my mirror, and she looks a lot like me,
Though theres lines around her eyes, and her hair is wild and free.
She is plumper than myself, and she definitely is grey.
Did I miss the day this happened? Has she always been this way?
And this woman in the mirror, has an air of something calm,
Like a tide that's going out, and a beach that's soft and warm.
She has seen the world in colour, she has learned to know the truth.
There's a wisdom in her wrinkles, there's a knowledge brought from youth,
And she seems to move more freely, as though released from earthly binds,
Is she made of something lighter? Perhaps the weight she left behind,
Like the press of expectations, and the need to yield and bend.
I like this woman in the mirror, she's fast becoming my best friend.

MY SENSE OF "ME" by Tanya

My sense of "me" is not defined by the opinions /descriptions of others – or past things that have happened to "me".

My sense of "me" is created by & cultivated by "me".

In the here & now I commit to the actions required to care for "me"… the self-care & soul-food I know I require to keep my body-mind & soul healthy.

How I treat "me" teaches others how to treat "me" & it demonstrates I value "me".

The boundaries I set reinforce how I require others to treat "me" & what I "will" & "will not" have in my life – which are my choices & my responsibility.

My sense of "me" holds my heart and soul in deep contentment and peace My sense of "me" is complete

'Gallery' Art and Photographs

- **'ART FROM THE 'HEALING BROKEN WINGS EXHIBITION'**

My Prison by Robyn

'Gallery' Art and Photographs

There is Always Light by Amy

Mask 'Survivor'

Group of Masks

'Empowerment' Vision Board

I Will Protect You by Shadi

• 'PHOTOS

**Tanya: Married at 19yo. 'I had no say, and
I hold no memories of this day'**

Tanya & daughter: The 'Zonta Education Award 2010' as I started my University study

'Gallery' Art and Photographs 159

Women's Circle

Healing Retreat in the Forest

Safe and Empowered Survivors: Tanya, Marney, Georgia, Lynette, Jordey

KEEPING US SAFE & STRONG PROGRAM

BASED ON SAFETEEN CANADA

Providing you with knowledge, skills and strategies to enhance your safety & minimise your risks in all situations

Hold Your Power and Speak Your Truth.

This is a pilot program for Pinjarra SHS Students, funded by the WA Police Community Crime Prevention Grant.

14 CAMP ROAD, PINJARRA | 9507 8534
SAFEWOMANSAFEFAMILYWA.COM
FIND US ON FACEBOOK AT SAFEWOMANSAFEFAMILYW.A.

The Keeping Us Safe School Program

Tanya receiving 'Australia Day Community Citizen Award' Shire of Murray, 2020

Tanya receiving 'UNAAWA Gender Equality Award' 2022

CHAPTER 14

Afterword

I sincerely hope you have gained benefit from reading this manual and if just one message you have received has resonated that will guide you on your path to being a **'Safe and Empowered Woman'**, for this I will be thankful.

My final hope is that to each of you ladies, regardless of your life's circumstances – you can awaken to the beautiful and unique *flame of light that resides within you* and that you have a right to a *'good and safe life'* so your flame can flourish.

Every one of us has the power to create **CHANGE** and move from the darkness to the light, and to create environments of security and safety by our deliberate actions and choices. No matter how small the steps are or how long it will take – **'Believe it and you can achieve it'** just as I did and so did the many women whose journeys I have witnessed over the years, and those who have shared their **'Stories of Hope and Inspiration'** within this Manual.

YOU DESERVE IT!
YOU ARE WORTH IT!

I look forward to hearing some of your Healing Journey Stories and welcome you to email them to me at iamwomanempowerment@gmail.com. If you would like individual assistance from me please reach out through the **Contact Me** section on my website and the same goes if you feel drawn to participate in either of my programs: https://www.iamwomanempowerment.com

If you send a photo of your book purchase receipt, I am providing a **25% Discount** off the cost of each program registration.

I would also like to offer you **FREE MEMBERSHIP** as a VIP Guest in my Private Facebook Group **'Safe and Empowered Women'** which is purely for those who have purchased the Manual or Programs. I will be doing a weekly **Live Chat Q&A** with regular guests. To register email as above with a photo of your book purchase receipt.

Warmest Regards & Best Wishes from Tanya

References

Anglicare WA (n.d.). *Services for parents after separation.* [Brochure]. West Australia. Author.

Australia's National Research Organization for Women's Safety. (ANROWS). *The 2018 Data Report from the Australian Domestic Violence Death Review.*

Australian Bureau of Statistics. (ABS). (2021-2022). *Personal Safety Australia.*

Australian Institute of Health and Welfare (AIHW). (2019a). *Family domestic and sexual violence in Australia: continuing the national story.*

Australian Institute of Health and Welfare (AIHW). (2021). (2022).

Berk, L.E. (2005). *Infants, Children and Adolescents (5thed).* Boston. Pearson Education Inc.

Biddulph, S. (1997). *Raising boys.* Finch publishing Pty Ltd. Lane Cove. NSW.

Bowlby, T. (1988). *A secure base: parent-child attachment and healthy human development.* New York: Basic Books.

Brecht, G. (1997). *Sorting out relationships.* Prentice Hall, Australia Pty Ltd.

Brogan, K., Laborg, K. (2016). *A mind of your own: The truth about depression and how women can heal their bodies to reclaim their lives.* Harper Collins. New York.

Campbell, A. (2023). *Bad to the bone.* Retrieved from https://www.justiceclearinghouse.com/resource/bad-to-the-bone-pet-abuse-child-abuse-and-intimate-partner-violence/

Western Australian Aids Council (n.d.). Consent Just Ask, [Booklet]. WA, Author.

Dart Institute. https://www.dartgroupaustralia.com.au/

Engel, B. (2006). *Healing your emotional self.* John Wiley & Sons Inc., Hoboken. New Jersey.

Fedders, L. (1999). *Women & Domestic Violence: An interdisciplinary approach.* New York: The Haworth Press.

Garbarino, J. (1985). *Adolescent development: An ecological perspective.* Columbus, Ohio: Charles E. Merrill Publishing Company.

Harvey, A., Garcia-Moreno, C., & Butchart, A. (2007). *Primary prevention of intimate partner violence and sexual violence:* Background paper for WHO expert meeting 2007.

Hay, L. (1988). *Heal your body.* Hay House, London. United Kingdom.

Heal for Life, (n.d.). *Heal for Life Foundation* [Booklet]. N.S.W., Author.

Heise, L., Garcia-Moreno, C. (2002). *Intimate partner violence.* In: *World report on violence and health.* Geneva, World Health Organization.

Hill, A.O., Bourne, A., McNair, R., Carman, M., & Lyons, A. (2020). *Private Lives: The health and wellbeing of LGBTIQ people in Australia.* Australian Research Centre in Sex, Health and Society, La Trobe University.

Hollander, J.A. (2018). *Empowerment Self Defence.* In Orchowski, L.M., Gidycz, C.A.. (Eds.), *Sexual assault risk protection: Theory, research and practice.* (pp. 221-224). Philadelphia.

Humphreys, C. (2007). A health inequalities perspective on violence against women. *Health & Social Care in the Community,* 15(2), 120-127.

Levesque, R.J.R. (2001). *Culture and family violence.* Washington: American Psychological Association.

Levine, P. (1997). *Waking the tiger.* North Atlantic Books. Berkeley, California, USA.

Moore, T. (2008). *Supporting young children and their families.* Retrieved from https://ww2.rch.org.au/emplibrary/ccch/Need_for_change_working_paper.pdf

Myss, C. (1996). *Anatomy of the spirit.* Harmony Books. New York.

National Centre on Domestic Violence, Trauma and Mental Health (NCDVT & MH) (2004). *Responding to domestic violence: Tools for Mental Health Providers.*

National Community Attitudes Towards Violence Against Women Survey. https://www.ncas.au/

Norwood, R. (2008). *Women who love too much.* Arrow Books. London.

Our Watch Australia. https://www.ourwatch.org.au/

PLAN International. https://www.plan.org.au/

Roberts, A. (2001). *Safe Teen.* Raincoast Books. Canada

Routt, G. & Anderson, L. (2015). *Adolescent violence in the home.* Routledge. New York.

Services Australia. https://www.servicesaustralia.gov.au/centrelink?context=1

The Victorian Royal Commission into Family Violence. https://www.vic.gov.au/ending-family-violence-annual-report-2021/royal-commission-into-family-violence

Trevillion, K., Oram, S., Feder, G., & Howard, L.M. (2012). *Experiences of Domestic Violence and Mental Health Disorders: A Systematic Review and Meta-Analysis, PLoS ONE, 7(12).*

Van Krieken, R., Habibis, D., Smith, P., Hutchins, B. & Holborn, M. (2006). *Sociology: Themes and perspectives (3rd ed.).* Frenchs Forrest, NSW: Pearson Education Australia.

Vaughn, C., Davis, E., Murdolo, A., Chen, J., Murray, L., Black, K., Quaizon, R., & Warr, D. (2016). *Promoting community led responses to violence against immigrant and refugee women. The Aspire Project.* Sydney, N.S.W. In ANROWS: (CFCA). 2018.

Western Australian Aids Council (n.d.). Consent Just Ask, [Booklet]. WA, Author.

World Health Organization (2009). *Violence against women.* Fact Sheet No 239, Geneva.

Zohre, A., Najman, J., & Williams, G. (2018). *Does leaving an abusive partner lead to a decline in victimization?* BMC Public Health, 18, Article Number: 404.

About the Author

Tanya Langford

Tanya Langford was born in England, and at the age of 7 with her parents and siblings migrated and settled in rural Western Australia. After finishing high school she studied to become a School Dental Therapist a role she continued in varied locations for several years. Her earlier passions were horse-riding and basketball.

Tanya navigated personal challenges in relationships and became keenly aware of the area of women's struggles, which began a curiosity and a desire for knowledge and pathways to help others who had experienced similar to her.

In 2009 as a single mother of two children, she committed herself to her goals and commenced university study. She graduated in 2012 with a Bachelor of Social Science with a Major in Welfare & Community Services, having put the focus of her studies on the field of gender-based violence and understanding the societal factors that contribute to this issue.

Since that time Tanya has assisted hundreds of women plus young people, firstly in her role as a Family Support Officer for a youth organization, and then in a charity organization she co-founded and ran, and in the past two years through her organization 'I Am Woman Empowerment Programs'. Tanya has created and facilitates a number of Recovery & Empowerment Programs which have successfully transformed many women's lives in overcoming trauma from all forms of violence and sexual abuse.

In addition, Tanya has conducted her own research in the area of 'AVITH' (Adolescent Violence in the Home) plus was actively involved with the RMIT University Project 'PIPA' (Positive Interventions in the Perpetration of Adolescent Violence in the Home).

In this time Tanya has received numerous accolades recognizing her commitment to supporting women and prevention of domestic violence. The most recent being the 2022 UNAAWA Gender Equality Award, in 2021 the Australia Day Community Citizen Award in The Shire of Murray and in 2016 the Perth Convention Bureau – City of Mandurah Aspire Award.

Tanya lives in Pinjarra, West Australia and looks forward to publishing her abuse prevention manual to fulfill her mission of using a preventive and early intervention approach to keeping girls and women safe from abuse and living their lives as Safe and Empowered Women.

Tanya's website and contact:
www.iamwomanempowerment.com
Email: iamwomanempowerment@gmail.com

Acknowledgements

I express my gratitude to every woman who has entrusted me to play a part in their journey of 'Healing and Recovery', and those who have shared my passion facilitating alongside me, and those who have been my Mentors and Guides.

I would like to acknowledge the contribution of Anita Roberts (Safeteen) in the Early Intervention Education for our Girls section of this Manual, and for the unwavering support she has shared with me these past several years.

TANYA LANGFORD

Tanya Langford (BSSc) is a Domestic & Family
Violence Consultant; Trauma Recovery & Empowerment
Life Coach & Author of 'The Domestic Abuse Prevention Manual'.

Tanya is also a survivor of the Cycle of Abuse & Violence which she experienced many years of her life. By combining her journey from 'Hopelessness to Success' with many fields of learning & practice experience over the past 15 years, she has created unique 'Recovery Programs' that have changed hundreds of women's lives, as well as an 'Early Intervention Program' for teen girls.
With a deep understanding of the societal issue of 'Gender Based Abuse' & her dedication to creating change in not only her life – but for others as well, she has recognized risk factors for women that can be addressed with the right education & skills. Tanya has a clear message she wishes to convey to women everywhere – 'Stop It Before It Starts, or From Happening Again'& follow these steps to become a 'Safe & Empowered Woman'.
Tanya is a passionate & engaging speaker.

Key Topics:
1. Understanding Gender Based Abuse through an Ecological Theory Lens.
2. The Early Intervention & Prevention Approach for our girls.
3. The Journey of Recovery to Empowerment.

Tanya lives in the Peel region of West Australia. To enquire about engaging Tanya as a Speaker for your next event or workshop, please contact her via email: iamwomanempowerment@gmail.com or phone 0411 792006 for availability & pricing.
https://www.iamwomanempowerment.com

Notes

Notes

www.ingramcontent.com/pod-product-compliance
Lightning Source LLC
Chambersburg PA
CBHW030037100526
44590CB00011B/246